FOREIGN AND DOMESTIC FIRMS IN CANADA

A Comparative Study of Financial Structure and Performance

Daniel M. Shapiro

Concordia University

BUTTERWORTHS

Toronto

The Butterworth Group of Companies:

Canada: Butterworth & Co. (Canada) Ltd., Toronto, Vancouver
United Kingdom: Butterworth & Co. (Publishers) Ltd., London,
Borough Green
Australia: Butterworth Pty. Ltd., Sydney, Melbourne, Brisbane
New Zealand: Butterworths of New Zealand, Ltd., Wellington
South Africa: Butterworth & Co. (South Africa) Pty. Ltd., Durban
United States: Butterworth Inc., Boston
Butterworth (Legal) Inc., Seattle

Canadian Cataloguing in Publication Data

Shapiro, Daniel M., 1947-
Foreign and domestic firms in Canada

Bibliography: p.
Includes index.

ISBN 0-409-86615-6

1. Business enterprises—Canada—Finance.
2. Business enterprises, Foreign—Canada—Finance. 3. Corporate
profits—Canada. I. Title.

HG4090.S52   338.6'041   C80-094284-1

33,817

Acknowledgements

I have accumulated many debts of gratitude in the course of completing this project. The study was begun as part of the research programme of the Anti-Inflation Board, but was completed after the AIB's demise. Access to the Statistics Canada data was arranged by the Anti-Inflation Board. The data were compiled and processed in the Business Finance Division of Statistics Canada with the able assistance of its staff, particularly Peter Blitt and Claude Methot. Many people, some who have remained anonymous to me, read and commented on the manuscript, in sections or in its entirety. I am particularly grateful to Nick Stosic for his generous assistance. The typing was done at Concordia University by Beverly Cobb, and the manuscript was given its final shape by Steve Andrews of Butterworths.

D. Shapiro
Montreal
March, 1980.

Preface

The extent to which foreign-controlled firms dominate key manufacturing and resource-based industries in Canada has been extensively documented and is well known to Canadians. Some 60% of these industries are foreign owned. It is therefore not surprising that the subject of foreign ownership has long been of interest to Canadians. Somewhat more surprising is the fact that no national consensus has emerged over the role of foreign-controlled firms in Canada, despite the many studies devoted to the issue, and the public debate which often ensued.

As multinational firms extend their international activities concern is being expressed in other countries, both developed and developing. However, both the long history and the high level of foreign ownership in Canada make the Canadian experience relevant to all who are interested in the phenomenon of foreign investment. It is hoped, therefore, that this study will contribute to a clearer definition and understanding of the issues, both in Canada and abroad.

I have tried to write a book which, while academic in orientation, can be read by more than a small circle of professionals in the field. Given the importance of the debate over foreign ownership, and the desirability of provoking wide-spread and informed discussion, the attempt to reach a wider audience is surely justified. Nevertheless, it has been necessary to rely on the professional literature, and to employ statistical methods, both of which may be unfamiliar to a general audience. However, anyone with a background in economics or business should be able to read the majority of the book. Chapters V and VI may be somewhat less accessible, but in all cases results are summarized in non-technical language. Upper-level undergraduate students in economics and/or business who have read parts of the book have experienced minimal difficulty in understanding most of what they read. As with all compromises, the approach pursued here may not satisfy all potential readers, but this could not be avoided.

The reader should be aware that although the study covers the period 1968-1972, and in this sense might be considered of historical interest only, the process of data collection, editing, and processing is such that it was not possible to examine the more recent past. Were this study to commence today, only data up to 1975 would be available, and by the time it appeared, it would seem equally dated. Such is the nature of studies of this type. I am convinced, however, that most of the results are representative and would not be altered in any substantive way by the inclusion of data for subsequent years.

Table of Contents

I

INTRODUCTION

The emergence of the multinational corporation (MNC) as an important element in the world economy has raised serious questions concerning the nature and effects of foreign investment and control. Nowhere in the developed world have these concerns been more widely expressed than in Canada, where the degree of foreign ownership is particularly high. As a consequence, a number of official studies have been commissioned to assess the extent, nature, and impact of foreign investment on the Canadian economy. Some legislation has resulted, notably the Corporations and Labour Unions Returns Act (CALURA), which empowers Statistics Canada to collect data related to foreign ownership, and the Act establishing the Foreign Investment Review Agency (FIRA), whose mandate is the screening of foreign take-overs of Canadian firms.

In spite of the considerable resources devoted to the study of foreign ownership, there are important areas where our knowledge remains limited. One such area is a comparison of foreign and domestic firms in Canada. While it is possible to draw some conclusions from aggregated, published data, such conclusions remain susceptible to aggregation biases. The only major study which compared foreign and domestic firms in Canada using firm-level data was that of Safarian (1966). Safarian used privately collected survey data for a limited sample of firms, the data being relevant to the late 1950s. He concluded that there were limited differences between foreign and domestic firms, and that those differences which did exist were often attributable to factors other than foreign ownership per se. Although there has been considerable progress made in the theory of MNC behaviour, Safarian's study remains unique in Canada, there having been no subsequent large-scale comparative studies of foreign and domestic firms in Canada.[1]

Recent surveys by Dunning (1973) and Lall (1978) indicate that the situation is the same in other countries. Few comparative studies of foreign and domestic firms exist, and most of these rely on relatively small data sets. The absence of information means that policy makers must rely on "generalizations drawn from scanty evidence, or, more commonly, on a priori beliefs about the behaviour and impact of TNCs."[2]

This study will partially fill this void by analysing and comparing the financial structure and performance of 750 of the largest domestically and foreign-controlled manufacturing firms in Canada. The data base was constructed by the author from previously unavailable financial and ownership data collected by Statistics Canada, and represents the largest and most reliable data set thus far available to Canadian researchers. The study covers the period from 1968 to 1972, these years having been determined by the availability of data. Chapter II is devoted to a discussion of the construction of the data set and its properties.

The first part of the study analyses financial structure. A firm's financial structure is defined by a series of financial ratios constructed from its balance sheet. Such ratios are defined and computed in Chapter III, and the financial structures of Canadian- and foreign-controlled firms are compared. Since differences in financial structure are thought to result from differences in firm conduct, ceteris paribus, this analysis can better our understanding of MNC behaviour.

The remaining chapters are devoted to firm performance. For the purposes of this study, performance will be defined by two variables: profitability and growth. Various measures of profitability are defined and examined in Chapter IV, and these measures are used to compare the level and stability of profitability of the ownership groups. A complete model of inter-firm differences in profitability is presented in Chapter V. Similarly, various measures of growth are defined in Chapter VI, and the comparative analysis of growth follows.

In order to give some precision to the subsequent analysis, we turn now to a discussion of the theory of the multinational corporation. The purpose of this discussion is to show that there are theoretical reasons for believing that the subsidiaries of multinational firms will not behave in the same manner as domestically controlled firms, owing to the nature of the MNC. The nature of the MNC and its conduct will therefore result in differences in economic performance. Before we proceed, a caveat is in order.

The firms in the sample are classified by country of control and the comparative analysis is thus based on comparing ownership or control groups. This does not necessarily coincide with the notion of a multinational corporation. For example, a firm may be classified as U.S.-controlled, but it may not be the subsidiary of a MNC. Similarly, a firm may be classified as Canadian-controlled, but may be a MNC. In theory, it is improper to equate all foreign-controlled firms with multinationals and all Canadian-controlled firms with non-MNCs. This problem could not be avoided; yet it is unlikely to represent a serious obstacle. For one thing, there are few Canadian MNCs, and a large percentage of these are foreign-controlled.[3] Of the Canadian-controlled MNCs, many are classified as mining or utilities, industries which are not represented in our sample. As will be seen in Chapter II, the firms in the sample are relatively large, which reduces the likelihood that a foreign-controlled firm is the subsidiary of a small, non-MNC parent. In practice, then, one can proceed on the assumption that foreign-controlled firms are related to MNCs, while Canadian-controlled firms are not.

According to Hymer (1960) and Caves (1971), firms invest abroad in order to capitalize on the ownership of some asset unique to the firm. The unique asset may be a process, a product, or an organizational technique, which must be transferrable to another country at zero (or very low) marginal cost. The uniqueness of the asset gives the firm some oligopolistic advantage which it transfers abroad. Possession of such assets are therefore usually in the hands of large firms with some market power. Since large firms are presumed to be large because there is some advantage to size, the movement abroad is also interpreted as an attempt to exploit scale economies at the firm level.[4] This latter view is associated in Canada with the work of Eastman and Stykolt (1967). They argue that firms will have more to gain from multi-plant operations if it is difficult to achieve an optimum size of plant, i.e., if existing plants are too small. Since the Canadian market is small, and is known to be populated by relatively small plants (Scherer, 1973) which are below minimum efficient scale, there is an inducement to multi-plant operations. While this holds for both Canadian and foreign-based firms, the latter have an advantage when they originate in a larger market and have already achieved large size.

The Hymer and Caves approach, while apparently similar to that of Eastman and Stykolt, does result in a different prediction regarding the relative profitability of Canadian and foreign-controlled firms. Eastman and Stykolt do not suggest that there will be differences in profitability, *ceteris paribus*, since both types of firm will attempt to maximize profits. In other words, when size is accounted for, Canadian and foreign-controlled firms should be equally profitable. Indeed, Safarian (1969) and the Watkins Report (1968) both failed to find any evidence that the subsidiaries of foreign-controlled firms were more profitable than their Canadian counterparts.

In the Hymer-Caves approach, the possession of a unique asset by the parent gives the subsidiary access to technology developed in the home market, to pools of managerial talent, and to patents, trademarks and brand names, all of which have been previously developed and are therefore available at zero marginal cost. In addition, subsidiaries have access to the financial resources of the parent, perhaps at preferential rates, and enjoy the reduced transactions and risk costs involved in avoiding market transactions in favour of non-arm's length transactions with the parent. This leads to the hypothesis that foreign-controlled firms will be more profitable than domestically controlled firms, ceteris paribus. In other words, even after size and market power have been accounted for, subsidiaries of MNCs should be more profitable. There is a return to 'multinationality' resulting from the access to an international system of information, sourcing and management. Evidence from the U.K. (Dunning, 1969) and Australia (Brash, 1966) tend to support this view.

There are other factors which should be accounted for. Caves (1975) reports that "the Canadian plants of multinational companies are more diversified than those belonging to domestically owned Canadian companies" (p. 4). If this diversification results in production runs which are too short, resulting in delays for re-tooling and breakdowns, then costs would be higher, and profits lower, ceteris paribus, for such firms. In other words, the 'miniature replica effect', whereby entire product lines are produced in the foreign market, may result in plants which are not sufficiently specialized. The consequence may be relatively higher costs for foreign-controlled subsidiaries. A related consideration, most often raised in the context of developing countries, is that of technological adaptation. If the original technology is not adapted to local conditions, but is merely scaled down for use in the host market, the result may be plants which are non-optimal in size. In addition, the scaling down of technology may result in errors so that the plant operates with under- or over-capacity. Although these problems are less likely to exist in a developed country such as Canada, Parry (1973), following the above logic, found that foreign-controlled firms in Australia operated with more excess capacity. Thus, there are arguments which suggest that foreign-controlled subsidiaries may incur additional costs which could make them relatively less profitable.

Of course, if the subsidiary is able to pass on the additional cost, then profitability would not be affected. This would be the case if foreign-controlled firms tended to cluster in industries where concentration and therefore market power was high, a possibility for which Rosenbluth (1970) could find no Canadian evidence. Nevertheless, the relationship between foreign control and industrial concentration is one which cannot be ignored in any examination of profitability. Accordingly, this issue is discussed in Chapter II.

It should be noted that measured concentration may underestimate the degree of interdependence amongst foreign-controlled firms in a given industry. It has been found that foreign investors tend to move abroad in bunches, this tendency being stronger the more concentrated is the industry in the investing country (Knickerbocker, 1973). Thus, in the case of a highly concentrated industry in the home market, an entire industry may move abroad, one firm after another, for competitive reasons. To the extent that industry-wide market sharing or pricing arrangements exist in the home market, these may be transplanted into the host country, regardless of the degree of measured concentration in that industry. Put another way, the well established interdependence of foreign oligopolists in one market may be transplanted to another market at the expense of domestic firms.

Considering the literature on MNCs as a whole, one cannot arrive at a definitive hypothesis regarding the relative profitability of foreign- and domestically controlled firms. On balance, however, the Hymer-Caves approach seems most persuasive, particularly for a country like Canada where the (potential) negative effects of technological adaptation seem unlikely to apply. In any event, it is evident that a study of comparative profitability must account for factors such as firm size and industrial concentration.

As a final note on profitability, it should be pointed out that the discussion thus far has ignored the temporal aspects of profitability, specifically its stability over time. There is no literature on the subject of the relative stability of profitability of foreign- and domestically controlled firms. It will therefore be approached as a purely empirical problem in Chapters IV and V.

Profitability and growth are usually linked (Eatwell, 1971). More profitable firms are expected to grow faster than less profitable firms because they can generate more internal funds and can borrow more externally. Can this logic be expected to apply when comparing the growth of foreign and domestic firms? If, for example, foreign-controlled firms are more profitable, can one necessarily expect them to grow faster? There are in fact certain independent considerations which suggest that the growth-profitability link may be less strong in the case of foreign-controlled subsidiaries.

It has been suggested that the movement abroad represents just one alternative in the growth process of the firm (Bertin, 1972, Wolf, 1978, Caves, 1975). As a firm saturates the domestic market for a particular product, its growth rate will begin to decline. In order to maintain its over-all growth rate (and its profit rate, under certain assumptions), the firm will begin to diversify. Diversification can assume several forms: new products, new industries or new markets. All of these represent different, and often mutually exclusive, policies designed to maintain the rate of growth of the firm. Thus, firms which diversify heavily in their home markets are less likely to invest abroad.

A subsidiary of a multinational firm will, after an appropriate lag, pass through the same product cycle, and the need for diversification will arise. However, there is every reason to believe that the reaction of the subsidiary will differ from that of the parent. The difference resides in the nature of the MNC, whose essential characteristic is the ability to move resources, specifically financial capital, to all parts of the world. Therefore, the subsidiary has an alternative to the types of diversification mentioned above: the remittance of profits to the parent for investment elsewhere in the parent system. Funds may be channelled via the parent to other countries whose market opportunities are relatively more attractive (perhaps because the parent has not yet penetrated such a market), or they can be used by the parent for diversification in the home market (including the development of new products). In the latter case, there may be a feedback effect to the host country in the form of new products and processes developed by the parent, and then transferred to the subsidiary.

In general, however, as a subsidiary matures one expects that rather than diversifying within the host country market, the firm will resort to increased remittances in various forms.[5] There is some evidence, to support the product- or firm-cycle view. Prachowny and Richardson (1975) have shown that remittances from subsidiaries do tend to increase with the age of the subsidiary. Caves (1975) has shown that the subsidiaries of U.S. firms operating in Canada are in fact less diversified than their parents, although the larger the subsidiary the more diversified it is likely to be. Thus, foreign subsidiaries tend to be truncated versions of their parents with the difference often being the centralization of research and development capabilities in the home country.

The data on U.S. foreign investment tend to confirm this view.[6] For manufacturing, the rate of profit and the rate of growth of sales of U.S. subsidiaries in Canada were declining relative to Europe over the period 1947-1972. Simultaneously, the rate of capital inflow to Canada has been declining relative to Europe. The rate of capital formation by U.S. manufacturing subsidiaries in Canada was lower than that in any country surveyed by the U.S. Commerce Department. The repatriation of funds through dividends, royalties and fees, and current receivables was increasing both relatively and absolutely until the point was reached in the sixties where, for the first time, there was a net outflow of U.S. funds from Canada. In contradistinction, there was a net inflow to Europe. One can interpret these findings as evidence that U.S. investment in Canada has reached a mature phase, and as a consequence funds are being channelled to newer and bigger markets, primarily in Europe.

These considerations suggest that subsidiaries of multinational corporations may not translate their profits into an expansion of the firm if the firm is in the mature stage of the product cycle, or if diversification possibilities are more attractive elsewhere. Unfortunately, it is difficult to identify and measure factors such as the degree of maturity of a firm and its products. In the context of the present study, no such measures were available. Thus, we must content ourselves with the identification of differences in the underlying growth processes of different ownership groups, even if the cause of such differences remains somewhat ambiguous. In Chapter VI the analysis of comparative growth is undertaken within the traditional context of Gibrat's Law applied to international business (see, for example, Rowthorn and Hymer, 1971).

It might be noted at this point that the growth process may differ not only between domestic and foreign-controlled firms, but amongst the latter as well. Firms which are relatively new to the Canadian market, such as the subsidiaries of German- or Japanese-based parents, may behave differently from U.S.-controlled firms, which are more likely to exhibit characteristics of maturity. Thus, the firms in the sample have been classified into three control categories: subsidiaries of U.S. firms, subsidiaries of other foreign firms, and Canadian-controlled firms. The analysis of growth, and of profitability and financial structure, will therefore use this tripartite division of the sample.

The nature of the MNC also raises questions regarding their financial behaviour, and the financial behaviour of their foreign affiliates. Do subsidiaries of foreign-controlled firms conform to host-country financial norms, or do they adopt financial norms established either in the home country of the parent or in the international financial market to which the parent may have access? The extent to which subsidiaries of MNCs are able to adopt financial strategies which differ from those of domestic firms will depend upon the degree of segmentation of international capital markets (including restrictions on capital flows in both home and host countries), the degree to which the parent is capable of integrated financial planning, and the extent to which the parent is forced to conform to financial norms established in its home market. In the case of a perfect international capital market, the last consideration would be unimportant, since shareholders in the home market would be indifferent about the method or source of finance. However, where international capital markets are not perfect, shareholders in the home market may resist efforts by the firms to borrow abroad (thus increasing the financial risk of the firm) if they themselves are prohibited from lending in such markets, either because of outright restrictions, or because of lack of information or excessive transactions costs. In this context it is apparent that capital markets may be more perfect for institutions than they are for individuals.

Robbins and Stobaugh (1974) have argued that the MNC and its subsidiaries should be considered as a profit-maximizing system, with a hierarchy of decision-making units. The head office of the MNC acts as a central planner of investment and finance decisions for its units throughout the world. To the extent that it is possible, headquarters attempts to centralize all sources of capital for dispersion to its various units. The interconnectedness of the elements of the system allow the firm a certain amount of financial flexibility which will be reflected in the balance sheets of its various subsidiaries. With the use of simulation models they show that profit-maximizing behaviour by the centre may result in apparently 'abnormal' financial behaviour by individual subsidiaries. Although they recognize that MNCs are not entirely free to move funds at will, Robbins and Stobaugh nevertheless believe that MNCs are able to avoid restrictions and impediments to capital flows, and they therefore reject the notion that capital markets are segmented. The larger is the MNC and the more sophisticated is its financial management, the more likely it will be that financial centralization will occur. In short, MNCs may be said to operate within internal capital markets.

In addition, of course, the very nature of the MNC suggests that these firms and their subsidiaries will have access to formal capital sources which are not available to other firms. Thus, Pattison (1978, p. 35) is led to the conclusion that the "operations of a foreign subsidiary in Canada are governed by many environmental concerns which are either very different from or unknown to Canadian firms."

While in principle it seems obvious that the financial environment of foreign subsidiaries will differ from that faced by domestic firms, the precise nature of the differences is difficult to specify, a priori. For example, there are conflicting tendencies regarding the use of debt by the foreign subsidiaries. One might expect them to rely heavily on debt financing, both long and short term, for a number of reasons: they can borrow in markets where interest rates are lower; they can borrow from their parent; and they may get preferential rates in the host market. In addition, it is generally believed that the parent will prefer to lend money to its affiliates rather than supply funds via new equity capital, since the former, being contractual, is easier to repatriate in the form of interest payments. Thus, subsidiaries may tend to be thinly capitalized. Furthermore, the use of debt incurred in the host country tends to minimize the risk of loss due to ex-change-rate changes, since the debt is denominated in local cur-rency. Robbins and Stobaugh indicate that subsidiaries are likely to carry greater current liabilities because they borrow short term in order to avoid exchange losses. In general, a subsidiary will attempt to maintain a net hard monetary position.

There are also reasons why a subsidiary might prefer to retain earnings. These include the consideration of withholding taxes, transfer costs, and tax deferrals. The use of retentions would mini-mize the use of debt as a source of funds, at least for long-run uses. Different national practices may also be important. Toy et al. (1974) have shown that U.S. firms tend to prefer internal to debt financing, as compared to European and Japanese firms. If the national stock markets consider these patterns to be "normal", then subsidiaries may adopt financial practices from their parents, and these may differ by ownership groups. Leftwich (1974) and Berlin (1971) have shown that manufacturing affiliates of U.S. MNCs were more levered than their parents, on average. Canadian affiliates, however, relied more heavily on internal financing than other affiliates, particularly those in Europe.[7] This suggests that host-country financial condi-tions may influence the behaviour of foreign-controlled subsidiaries, but the extent may differ from country to country. Thus, one expects that the use of debt and retained earnings by the subsidiaries of MNCs may differ from that of domestic firms, but there may also be differences amongst affiliates, depending on the nationality of the parent. As a further complication, it appears that the subsidiaries of U.S. firms do not behave in the same manner in all countries.

Foreign-controlled firms may differ in other respects as well. Rob-bins and Stobaugh suggest that owing to sophisticated cash-manage-ment techniques, combined with a desire to mass cash reserves at the centre, subsidiaries will operate with below-"normal" cash re-serves (including short-term securities). One might therefore hy-pothesize that foreign-controlled firms will be less liquid than do-mestic firms. This liquidity effect, combined with the possible tendency for foreign-controlled firms to incur short-term debt, would result in a relatively worse net short-term position for foreign-controlled firms.

Robbins and Stobaugh also point out that since subsidiaries tend to export to, and import from, their parents, they are likely to maintain higher-than-average inventories in order to avoid delays in shipments due to customs delays and other problems related to inter-country flows of goods. This tendency would be exacerbated if transfer pricing was used to remit funds, thus causing subsidiaries to hold over-priced inputs as inventories. The desire to remit funds may also affect the receivables position of subsidiaries of foreign-based firms. When the remittance of funds via visible channels such as dividends is undesirable, subsidiaries may rely on transfer pricing, or the extension of credits to the parent. The latter is considered a common form of repatriation and would tend to inflate the receivables of firms engaging in such behaviour. Robbins and Stobaugh point out that only one half of remissions is through dividends; this suggests that other forms are not unimportant to the MNC.

Given the above discussion, one is led to the conclusion that the financial structure of foreign-controlled firms will differ from that of domestic firms, and that the differences will appear in a wide variety of financial items. Furthermore, it is possible that differences will exist amongst foreign-controlled firms themselves, depending on their country of origin. It must be pointed out, however, that the preceding analysis was very general, and designed to apply to all countries, including developing countries. Indeed, many of the conclusions are likely to apply more strongly to such countries than to a country like Canada. For example, financial manipulation to avoid stringent control of profit remissions, to offset currency restrictions, or to prevent losses from currency devaluation is less likely to occur in Canada than in a developing country.

It is rather strange, therefore, that Lall (1978) reports little evidence to suggest that financing practices of MNCs in developing countries are different from those of domestic firms, while Pattison (1978) finds rather major differences between domestic and foreign-controlled firms in Canada. Furthermore, some of Pattison's results do not confirm some of the hypotheses entertained above. For example, Pattison finds that foreign-controlled firms are more liquid than domestic firms in Canada, which is contrary to the hypothesis of Robbins and Stobaugh. Pattison also found that foreign-controlled firms tended to rely less on debt, and more on internal financing than did domestic firms. In general, he concludes that the financial structure of foreign-controlled firms is sounder than that of Canadian-controlled firms.

Pattison's results cannot be considered to be definitive, since he used aggregated data, and could not control for other factors which might affect a firm's financial structure, such as firm size. Thus, a more detailed analysis is called for, and that is the purpose of

Chapter III of this study. There, a comparative analysis of financial structures will be undertaken using firm-level data, and in a context where factors other than foreign control may be accounted for.

The issues raised by a comparative study of financial structure go beyond the nature of the MNC. They have important consequences for the host economy.[8] The widespread use of retained earnings as a source of funds by foreign-controlled firms (which Pattison finds for Canada) is thought to be undesirable for two reasons. First, it may hamper the effectiveness of monetary policy since firms do not rely on external sources of credit, and second, it might cause a misallocation of investment funds since firms will be able to avoid the discipline imposed by capital markets. The evidence on these matters is sparse and often conflicting, depending on the methodology employed and the country to which it is applied. Perhaps more important is the relative liquidity and leverage (debt) structures of foreign and domestic firms. If it is true that Canadian-controlled firms are less liquid and more highly levered (rely more on debt), the consequent financial risk may put them at a relative disadvantage. A financially risky firm may have difficulty in borrowing funds, particularly when financial institutions are either conservative or are unable to assess risk. Canadian financial institutions are often characterized in this way, which raises the possibility that financial markets may not work to the advantage of Canadian-controlled firms. In addition, less liquid firms tend to be most severely affected by restrictive monetary policy, particularly if credit rationing results. Such firms may have trouble raising short-term capital, and will be forced to rely on trade credits, a situation which might permit them to be squeezed by creditors. Lastly, financially risky firms may be susceptible to bankruptcy or takeover, a situation which could increase foreign ownership if the financially risky firms are Canadian-controlled.

This completes the survey of theoretical considerations relevant to this study. An examination of the nature of the MNC and of the environment in which it, and its subsidiaries, operate clearly suggests that there are likely to be important differences between these subsidiaries and comparable domestic firms. It remains to be seen whether the theoretical differences are empirically verifiable.

Notes

1. There have been studies which introduced foreign ownership as an explanatory factor when considering various aspects of firms' behaviour, thus implicitly comparing foreign- and Canadian-controlled

firms. A notable example is Howe and McFetridge's (1976) study of R & D expenditures by firms operating in Canada.

2. Lall (1978, p. 217). TNCs are trans-national corporations, the term that Lall prefers.

3. Pattison (1978) reports that in 1972 there were 38 Canadian firms listed in the Fortune 500 list of the largest non-U.S. industrials. Of these, 16 were foreign-controlled.

4. Note, however, that the scale economies may be real or pecuniary.

5. Here one should distinguish diversification at the plant level from diversification at the firm level. The former concerns the number of products produced in a plant (its specialization), while the latter concerns various activities undertaken by the firm (R & D, marketing).

6. The discussion which follows is based on data collected by the author and Luciano Coutinho (Shapiro, 1974 and Coutinho, 1975). The source of the data is the U.S. Commerce Department, *Survey of Current Business*, various issues, 1947-1974.

7. Furthermore, for all U.S. affiliates, there was a negative relationship between capital accumulation and the use of internal funds (Berlin, 1971), which emphasizes the crucial role of external financing in subsidiary expansion.

8. The discussion in this paragraph draws heavily from Pattison (1978, pp. 30-35).

II

THE DATA:
SOURCES AND
CHARACTERISTICS

II-1 Introduction

The process of constructing a data base is an important part of any research project. This is particularly true when firms are the object of analysis since sample size and composition, data sources, and definition of variables tend to differ from study to study. When more than one year is analysed, the possibility exists that the data and the sample are inconsistent from one year to the next, even within a given study. Thus, it is necessary to carefully document the procedures followed in constructing the data base so that the reader may judge the degree to which the conclusions are relevant. Section II-2 is devoted to this purpose.

Section II-3 provides some information regarding the general economic environment during the sample period (1968-1972). This is followed in Section II-4 by a presentation of some characteristics of the sample, specifically the relationship among firm size, industrial concentration, and foreign control. These relationships are summarized in Section II-5.

II-2 The Sample

The data used for this study were drawn from corporation financial statistics collected under the Corporations and Labour Unions

Returns Act (CALURA) and published in various aggregated forms in the annual CALURA report published by Statistics Canada. This study represents the first attempt to use these data on a cross-section corporate level. All confidentiality requirements of the Statistics Act are met by this cross-section analysis which treats each firm as an anonymous observation in a statistical program.

The data are stored in the form of a stylized balance sheet, standardized by the Business Finance Division, and include standard items such as assets, liabilities, revenues, deductions, and capital expenditures, all broken down into considerable detail for each year. For the purposes of this study, 50 financial variables were extracted for each firm in each year. (See the Appendix to this chapter.) The variables were chosen on the basis of the needs of this study.

In several cases, desired items were excluded owing to their non-availability in some years. In an effort to improve their coverage and accuracy, the Business Finance Division has revised and expanded its balance sheet from year to year so that some items are not available in all years. One notable example for the purposes of this study is the item "deferred taxes" which was only broken down as a separate item beginning in 1970 and is therefore excluded from the list of variables. Nevertheless, the 50 included variables provide a comprehensive data base.

In addition, each corporation is assigned a control code indicating the country of ultimate control, and an ownership ratio, representing the percentage of voting stock which is non-resident owned. In general, corporations which are more than 50% non-resident owned are defined as foreign-controlled, and are then assigned to a country where ultimate control is exercised. In a few cases firms are deemed to be foreign-controlled with lower than 50% non-resident ownership if substantial evidence is available to suggest that control is nevertheless exercised from abroad.[1]

The CALURA control codes include Canada, the United States, and several other countries. For the purposes of this study, the latter have been grouped into one. Thus there are 3 control categories: U.S., Canada, and Other Foreign. While the CALURA control codes are employed here, it is not done without reservation. It has been generally accepted since Berle and Means' (1932) classic study that effective control can be exercised by groups owning less than 50% of the voting shares of the firm. Some have suggested that control may be exercised through the ownership of as little as 5% of voting shares (see Zeitlin, 1974). The problem of ascertaining where the control of any corporation lies is a complex one, involving economic theory, the theoretical notion of what control means, and the practical problems involved in agreeing to, and implementing a definition of control. These problems are exacerbated in the case of affiliates of multinational firms where nominee holdings, pyramiding and inter-locking directorates may guarantee control by a foreign firm with very little ownership. In addition, vertical or horizontal integration across national boundaries may give MNCs some control over firms in which they have little stock ownership through long-term pur-chase and marketing agreements, franchising and licensing. Thus, it is likely that the CALURA definition of foreign control represents an understatement of the extent to which it actually exists. It was diffi-cult to avoid this problem, and in some cases the control code was replaced by the non-resident ownership (NRO) ratio.

Each corporation is further classified into a 3-digit SIC industry according to the industry in which the majority of its sales are made. This procedure also introduces some error since some corporations do substantial amounts of business in several SIC categories. It is im-possible to ascertain how much inaccuracy this involves, although it no doubt declines with the breadth of the SIC classification. As con-fidentiality requirements dictated that firms be aggregated into 2-digit industries, this problem is likely to be relatively insignificant.

The above information was available from CALURA. Outside data were then added to aid the analysis. Two measures of industrial con-centration were employed, both of which were derived from mate-rial published by Statistics Canada.[2] The first measure used was the Herfindahl index, published for each 3-digit industry. Each firm was assigned a Herfindahl Index (HERF) corresponding to the 3-digit in-dustry to which it belonged. The second measure was a set of dummy variables indicating whether the firm belonged to a 3-digit industry characterized by high (H), medium (M), or low (L) concen-tration levels. The criterion for assignment was based on the four- and eight-firm concentration ratios (C4, C8) for 3-digit industries as published in the cited report. Each 3-digit industry was classified as a high concentration industry if C4, C8 ≥ 70%, as a medium concen-tration industry if 70% > C4, C8 > 30% and a low concentration in-dustry if C4, C8 ≤ 30%. In the few cases where the classification as-signed to C4 and C8 differed (e.g., C4 = 25%; C8 = 40%), reference was made to the Herfindahl index and judgment was exercised in the assignation. In the cases where C4 and C8 were not published (HERF was available for all 3-digit industries) exclusive use of the Herfindahl Index was made. In all, 16 out of 139 industries involved elements of judgment. The relationship between the two measures is discussed below.

Each industry was further classified by product. A tripartite clas-sification scheme was employed according to whether a good was a producer good (P) a consumer-convenience good (C) or a consumer non-convenience good (N). The latter two categories were taken from the work of Porter (1974) who found that for the United States, industry performance differed according to product type. The difference between the two consumer-good categories is related to the method of retailing, with consumer-convenience goods being sold in retail outlets where face to face contact with a sales representative is rare and where the consumer may not compare prices among stores. Consumer non-convenience goods, on the other hand, are characterized by the interaction between consumer and sales representative, as well as by "shopping around" for the best price.

One outside variable which figures prominently in discussions of costs and profitability in Canada is the tariff (see Eastman and Stykolt, 1967 and Bloch, 1974). Unfortunately, detailed tariff data for the 139 3-digit industries represented could not be found and the tariff per se has been omitted. Our present knowledge, however, suggests that the tariff has only a marginal effect on profitability (Jones, et al., 1973 and McFeteridge, 1973), or that it acts in concert with concentration measures to affect profitability (Bloch, 1974). Furthermore, it now appears that foreign-owned firms are not necessarily found in high tariff industries (Caves, 1974 and Orr, 1975), and that any bias in the analysis caused by the omission of the tariff will affect Canadian- and foreign-owned firms in a similar manner. Thus, any differences found between Canadian- and foreign-controlled firms should not be attributed to the tariff.

Nevertheless, it was felt that the tariff should at least be partially accounted for. It was therefore decided to include industry dummy variables in the regression analyses. Since it was unrealistic to have a dummy variable for each of 139 3-digit industries, these were collapsed into 13 industry groupings, conforming more or less to a 2-digit system. These 13 industry groups were constructed in order to minimize statistical complications and satisfy the confidentiality requirements of Statistics Canada.[3] It is felt that if other factors are correctly accounted for in the models which follow, then these dummy variables should capture at least some of the effects of the tariff.

The study is confined to manufacturing corporations over the period 1968-1972. The choice of industries was made because the manufacturing sector is more easily put within the context of economic theory, and because of its obvious importance in any economy. The inclusion of resource and financial industries would have introduced problems relating to their unique circumstances.

The choice of years was dictated by considerations of data availability and compatibility. A base year of 1968 was chosen because pre-1968 data were not fully compatible with those for subsequent years; the data system had undergone substantial revision in that year. At the time this file was assembled, there were no data going beyond 1972, which (naturally) determined the terminal year. Subsequently, more recent data have become available, but their inclusion in the sample was not possible.

The choice of a sample is nearly as important as the analysis performed on it. For this reason great care was taken in selecting the sample firms, and the process was painstaking and time-consuming. It was desirous to produce a sample which was manageable, significant in size and impact, and unbiased. In order to satisfy the first two criteria, it was decided to concentrate on only the largest manufacturing firms. The chosen cut off point was $5 million and over in assets. The cut off point was not arbitrarily chosen, as Statistics Canada provides complete coverage for firms with over $5 million in assets and surveys smaller firms. This provided a potential sample of some 1000 firms which accounted for about 80% of manufacturing assets, depending on the year.

The next decision involved the choice of a base year on which to select the sample. It is known that this procedure can affect the results of a statistical analysis. For example, if 1968 was chosen as the base year, and if asset-size of $5 million and over in that year was the cutoff, then the sample would be biased against fast growing (and perhaps profitable) firms. This is so because a firm excluded in 1968 may well have grown so quickly as to be larger than an included firm in 1972. If 1972 was chosen as the base year, then both firms would have been included in the sample. In order to alleviate this bias, the following procedure was adopted.

The year 1968 was designated as the base, in the sense that all control codes, non-resident ownership ratios, and SIC classifications were based on 1968 data. A basic list of firms of asset-size exceeding $5 million was drawn up. These firms were then matched with the 1972 list of firms *in its entirety* to ensure that the firm was still in operation, even if its assets had declined to below $5 million. At this point the basic list was augmented by firms which, in 1972, had assets which were greater than or equal to the assets of the smallest firm already on the list in that 3-digit industry, provided that it exceeded $5 million in assets. For example, assume that a firm in SIC group 333 had assets of $5 million in 1968 and was thus included in the sample. By 1972 it had grown to $6 million. In both years it was the smallest firm in SIC 333 in the sample. The 1972 list was then scanned for firms of over $6 million in assets which were not on the 1968 list, and if such firms were found they were added to the list. The same procedure was followed if the firm did not grow, or declined in size. The process was then reversed, and the 1968 list was scanned to ensure that those firms added from the 1972 list existed in 1968. Since their assets were below $5 million in 1968, every firm so added was not found, since firms of under $5 million are only sampled by Statistics Canada. Thus, some firms were lost as a consequence of not being sampled. Some firms were lost as a result of being born after 1968, i.e., they existed in 1972, but not in 1968. This was a rare occurrence for firms of this size.

The sample remained inconsistent on a year to year basis owing to the inclusion of firms which merged with other firms. Such firms represent discontinuities in the data base owing to asset revaluations, stock splitting, etc. The balance sheets are simply not comparable from one year to the next, and for all intents and purposes they are new firms. The following procedures were therefore adopted:

(a) if the firm was born in 1970-1972, or if it died in 1969-71, or if it merged with an unrelated firm in years 1969-1971, it was deleted from the sample;

(b) if the firm merged with a related firm in 1969-71, the firms were treated as one firm for the entire period 1968-72, unless evidence indicated that this provided inconsistent data;

(c) if the firm was born in 1969, or if it died in 1972, or if it merged with any firm in 1968 or 1972, it was included for a four-year period, 1968-1971, or 1969-1972.

This procedure resulted in the addition of some firms which had not been found in the basic match of 1968 and 1972 firms. However, the number of recorded mergers increased dramatically toward the end of the period, and these included mergers between some very large firms.[4] The adopted procedure allowed most of these firms to remain in the sample, with a few exceptions. The most important exceptions were in the forest products and wood industries. Thus, relative to other industries, these two are somewhat under-represented in the sample. In addition to mergers, the forest products and wood industries were characterized by liquidations, consolidations, and entry of new firms.

There were other deletions made, as well. Newspapers were eliminated from the sample, as it was felt that they were not really comparable to other firms in the sample. Indeed, over the period several of them were reclassified from manufacturing to other industry groups (usually financial). This type of reclassification also resulted in the elimination of other firms who converted from production to holding-company status.

Lastly, there were some miscellaneous deletions which occurred when a firm existed as a legal entity, but was found to be dormant or, when for some other reason, unusual data characteristics were discovered. This latter group usually involved other foreign (non-American) firms which often ceased operations within a relatively short period. Some subsequently resumed operations. It is presumed that this occurs because the movement of such firms into Canada is recent, and there may be problems of adjusting to a new economic environment.

The final list therefore comprised 750 continuing manufacturing firms: 290 Canadian, 362 American, and 98 Other Foreign. A breakdown of these firms by the major industry grouping employed by CALURA is found in Table II-1. The size characteristics of the sample are found in Table II-2.

While it is not possible to know with certainty, it is felt that the three criteria for choosing the sample have been met. The sample is large in number and is composed of most of Canada's largest manu-

TABLE II-1

Sample Composition by Control and Industry

	U.S.	Canada	Other Foreign	Total
1. Food	31	39	9	79
2. Beverages	7	29	1	37
3. Tobacco Products	4	2	4	10
4. Rubber Products	9	1	2	12
5. Leather and Textiles	16	23	3	42
6. Knitting and Clothing	4	12	0	16
7. Wood	11	25	2	38
8. Furniture	3	6	0	9
9. Paper and Allied Products	20	37	13	70
10. Printing and Publishing	7	10	2	19
11. Primary Metals	16	16	9	41
12. Metal Fabricating	39	27	7	73
13. Machinery	41	8	8	57
14. Transportation Equipment	36	22	7	65
15. Electrical Products	32	10	4	46
16. Non-Metallic Minerals	9	10	11	30
17. Petroleum and Coal	13	0	3	16
18. Chemicals	45	8	12	65
19. Miscellaneous	29	5	1	25
TOTAL	362	290	98	750

TABLE II-2

Sample Composition by Size Class (Assets)

(dollars)

		U.S.	Canada	Other Foreign	Total
1.	<5,000,000	20	15	2	37
2.	5,000,000- 10,000,000	137	123	26	286
3.	10,000,000- 20,000,000	78	61	25	164
4.	20,000,000- 40,000,000	53	36	15	104
5.	40,000,000- 80,000,000	37	24	19	80
6.	80,000,000-160,000,000	19	18	7	44
7.	>160,000,000	18	13	4	35
	TOTAL	362	290	98	750

facturing firms (depending on the year chosen). Since approximately 20% of all manufacturing assets are accounted for by firms with assets of less than $5 million, and taking note of the fact that the sample does include 37 firms with less than $5 million in assets, it can be safely asserted that only an additional 5%-10% of total manufacturing assets have been deleted owing to the procedure outlined above. Thus, the sample represents between 70% and 75% of manufacturing assets.

In spite of its size, the data base is statistically manageable. Furthermore, the yearly data are consistent and the sample is relatively unbiased since a combination of base years was used.

In summary, a continuous sample of 750 of the largest manufacturing firms in Canada has been assembled for the period 1968-1972. For each firm in each year 50 financial items have been entered in a matrix. In addition, each firm is assigned a country of control code, a degree of non-resident ownership ratio, a 3-digit SIC number, a 2-digit SIC category, a Herfindahl index, a concentration dummy, and a product-type dummy.

We now proceed to a further evaluation of the sample period and some characteristics of the sample firms.

II-3 The Sample Period (1968-1972)

This section will provide a brief overview of the financial situation in Canada and the U.S. over the sample period. This information will prove to be useful in the subsequent analysis. Rather than reproduce financial statistics, comparative statements will be made, and the sources cited. The situations in Europe and Japan have been neglected because similar data sources were not available. We begin with the Canadian economy.

For all Canadian industries, the period 1968-1972 represented a U-shaped financial cycle. All profitability measures (on assets, equity or sales) declined from 1968 to 1970 (the trough) and rose thereafter, usually surpassing 1968 levels by 1972.[5] Efficiency (turnover) measures followed the same pattern. The period was also characterized by a secular decline in liquidity measures (current and quick ratios) and in debt-equity ratios.

As 1970 is generally thought to be the trough of a general business cycle, it may be concluded that Canadian industries reflected the course of the business cycle in their financial performance, with the exception of apparently continuing liquidity problems. These general trends conceal considerable diversity amongst industries.[6] Not only are there differences in the levels of various financial ratios among industries, but different industries follow different cyclical patterns.

The situation in the U.S. was somewhat similar over the period. The major difference was that the recovery in the U.S. following the 1970 trough was not as robust, at least according to profitability measures. According to U.S. sources, all profit rates declined from 1968 to 1970, but the pattern thereafter was mixed.[7] After-tax profits (on equity or sales) rose from 1970 to 1972, but did not reach 1968 levels, as was the case in Canada. Furthermore, the increase from 1970 to 1971 was modest. This result confirms the belief that Canadian profits exhibit a greater amplitude over the course of the business cycle than do U.S. profits.

Another observed difference was that the liquidity ratios for U.S. non-financial corporations followed the U-shaped pattern, whereas in Canada they declined steadily. A perusal of these published ratios indicates that on the whole, U.S. industries were more profitable than Canadian industries, and had lower degrees of leverage. This is by no means a scientific statement, but rather an impressionistic one. The ratios observed were based on different definitions and accounting procedures, and no correction was made for the exchange rate.

The five-year sample period is therefore characterized by both a downswing and an upswing, with a trough in 1970. However, there were differences between Canada and the U.S. in the levels and trends of financial indicators over the period. This is important to the extent that U.S. subsidiaries in Canada conform or react to U.S. financial norms or trends. This background information will prove to be useful in subsequent chapters.

II-4 Size, Concentration, and Foreign Ownership

In this section we analyse the relationships among firm size, industrial concentration, and foreign ownership. It is widely believed that foreign-controlled firms tend to be much larger than Canadian-controlled firms, and tend to be found in industries which are highly concentrated and where monopoly power can therefore be exercised. These beliefs, particularly the first, are based on data pertaining to all firms in Canada, both large and small. Since the very smallest firms are predominately Canadian-controlled, it is observed that foreign-controlled firms are on average larger than Canadian-controlled firms. In this study such small firms are not included in the sample, and the question to be examined is whether a size disparity between foreign- and Canadian-controlled firms exists when only larger firms are considered.

There is no particular agreement about the correct measure of firm size. The measure chosen is often dictated by data availability or by the type of analysis undertaken. The two most commonly used measures are the value of sales or assets of the firm. For the purposes of this study, asset-size was deemed a preferable measure since it is less likely to be influenced by market conditions and price fluctuations. Furthermore, asset size is employed in official publications such as the CALURA Reports, and its use in this study facilitates comparisons. Nevertheless, sales measures have been computed for comparative purposes. The logarithm of size is also useful for certain purposes since it compares proportionate rather than absolute size. When relatively large firms are being compared, the effects of size are more likely captured by the number of times larger one firm is than another, rather than by the number of dollars larger it is. The sales and assets measures have been averaged over the entire five-year period, and calculated separately for each of the five years. For reasons to be described in the sequel, it is sometimes necessary to use opening size rather than average size as the appropriate size measure. For this reason, we have calculated the size measures for 1968, and this is referred to as opening size. There are therefore, many possible measures of firm size, some of which are presented in Table II-3.

Table II-3 contains some surprising results. Although it is clear that U.S. and Other Foreign firms are larger than Canadian-controlled firms on average, as one would expect, these differences are not significant when assets or opening assets are used to measure size.[8] When the logarithm of assets is used, Other Foreign firms are

TABLE II-3

Size Variables

(dollars)

Variable	Country	Mean	Standard Deviation
Opening Size	U.S.	41,866	11,628
(Assets)	OF	44,719	90,229
(000)	CAN	34,952	80,096
	TOTAL	39,174	10,029
Average Size	U.S.	47,046	12,904
(Assets)	OF	48,933	100,797
(000)	CAN	39,657	89,501
	TOTAL	44,358	11,413
Opening Size	U.S.	48,225[2, 3]	14,640
(Sales)	OF	30,304[1]	66,409
(000)	CAN	30,167[1]	63,874
	TOTAL	38,901	11,206
Average Size	U.S.	54,442[2, 3]	16,527
(Sales)	OF	34,899[1]	78,084
(000)	CAN	35,706[1]	78,974
	TOTAL	44,161	12,822
Log Size	U.S.	9.72[2]	1.13
(Average-	OF	10.00[1, 3]	1.12
Assets)	CAN	9.69[2]	1.11
	TOTAL	9.77	1.30

Notes: 1 = significantly different from U.S. (at 5%)
  2 = significantly different from OF (at 5%)
  3 = significantly different from CAN (at 5%)

Significance levels are based on two-tailed t-tests which do not assume equal variances among the groups.

found to be significantly larger than either Canadian- or U.S.-controlled firms. However, Canadian- and U.S.-controlled firms are found not to be different from each other.

When sales is employed, it is found that U.S.-controlled firms are significantly larger than either Other Foreign- or Canadian-controlled firms, and that these are not different from each other. It should be noted that there is a strong relationship amongst all the measures of size. The correlation matrix presented in Table II-4 shows that asset and size measures are positively and significantly related so that over-all, a ranking of firms by asset size is similar to a ranking by sales size. For this reason, the use of either variable in the context of a statistical analysis would likely produce similar results.

TABLE II-4

Correlation Matrix

Size Measures

	Opening Size (Assets)	Opening Size (Sales)	Average Size (Assets)	Average Size (Sales)
Opening Size (Assets)	1.000	.778 (.001)	.996 (.001)	.769 (.001)
Opening Size (Sales)		1.000	.693 (.001)	.994 (.001)
Average Size (Assets)			1.000	.763 (.001)
Average Size (Sales)				1.000

n = 750 (bracketed terms are significance levels)

While we have seen that foreign-controlled firms are on average larger than Canadian-controlled firms (even though the difference is not always signficant), the use of averages can be misleading because they ignore the effect of industry on firm size. In the present context, we wish to determine whether the observed larger size of foreign-controlled firms results from their being larger in every industry, or from their being concentrated in industries where average firm size is higher.

In order to examine this question, the following regression equation was estimated:

$$\text{Size} = a + \sum_{i=1}^{12} b_i \ \text{Industry} + \sum_{j=1}^{2} c_j \ \text{Country}$$

Size is represented by the measures discussed above (assets, sales) and industry is represented by a series of dummy variables which = 1 if the firm is in that industry, = 0 if not. There are 13 industries in all, as described in Section II-2 above. The country variable represents the country of control and is also represented by dummy variables = 1 if the firm is controlled by the country, = 0 if not. There are 3 control groups (CAN, U.S., OF). For econometric reasons, it is necessary to omit one dummy variable from each set. In this case the Miscellaneous Manufacturing and Other Foreign control groups were omitted, leaving 12 industry and 2 control dummies. As a consequence, the constant term in the estimated equation assumes a special value; it is the average value of the dependent variable (size) for an OF firm in the Miscellaneous Manufacturing Industry.

This equation therefore separates industry from country of control as factors affecting firm size. It should be mentioned that this equation is not derived from a model, and is not designed to be explanatory, but is simply descriptive. Thus, this procedure begs the question of industry ownership structure. It cannot explain why foreign-controlled firms are found in some industries in greater number than in others, or why, for example, large Canadian-controlled petroleum firms are under-represented in that industry.

The following is an example of the type of equation which results.

Size (assets) = 20.9 − 3.5 Food and Beverages − 6.4 Clothing and Textiles − 6.7 Wood + 55.3* Pulp and Paper + 67.7* Primary Metals − 10.3 Metal Fabricating − 2.1 Machinery + 20.7 Transportation Equipment + 2.2 Electrical + 6.9 Non-metallic Minerals + 286.7* Petroleum + 1.0 Chemicals + 7.2 U.S. + 6.4 Canada

$\bar{R}^2$ = .18

F   = 11.91*

(14,735)

* = significant at 5%

In this case the constant has a value of 20.9 (million) which means that the average size of an Other Foreign firm in Miscellaneous Manufacturing is about $21 million in assets. Values for other industries and control groups are readily obtained by adding (subtracting) the relevant terms. For example, the average size of a U.S. firm in the food and beverages industry would be 20.9 − 3.5 + 7.2 = 24.6. A similar procedure would result in the average size of any industry-control combination.

In the above example, it is to be noted that the values of the coefficients for food and beverages (industry) and for U.S. firms (country) cannot be said to differ from zero (i.e., they are statistically insignificant). Thus, statistically, there is no difference in average size between a firm in a miscellaneous industry and one in food and beverages, regardless of the country of control.

In general, it can be seen that the coefficients for U.S. and Canadian firms are not significant and thus we can say that U.S. firms are not significantly larger than Canadian firms, even when industry is controlled for, and when size is measured in assets. Only three industry coefficients are significant: pulp and paper, primary metals, and petroleum. In each case the sign of the coefficient is positive indicating that firms in these industries are, on average, larger. When the petroleum industry is analysed we observe that its coefficient is some 4 times larger than the other two. Of the 16 petroleum firms in the sample, 13 are U.S.-controlled and 3 are OF-controlled. Thus, U.S. and OF firms are larger on average, primarily because they dominate the petroleum industry where the average size of firm is the highest in manufacturing.

When sales is considered as a measure of size, and a similar equation is estimated, the result is that the U.S. coefficient is significant and positive. U.S. firms are significantly larger than Canadian or Other Foreign firms when size is measured by sales and when industry is controlled for. This result indicates that when firm size is measured by sales, U.S. firms tend to be larger in any industry. Indeed, when industry averages are examined, Canadian-controlled firms are found to be larger in a majority of industries when assets is used as a measure of size; when sales is used to measure size U.S.-controlled firms are larger in a majority of industries.

The reconciliation of these findings is not the purpose of this chapter. Nevertheless, it seems obvious that U.S.-controlled firms are more efficient in their use of capital, i.e., that they have higher sales/assets ratios in any given industry. This point will be taken up in Chapter III.

For the remainder of this study, firm size will be measured in assets, and the term "size" will refer to asset-size unless otherwise specified.

We may now proceed to a discussion of the relationship among size, foreign ownership, and industrial concentration. It will be recalled that two measures of concentration were included in the data base: the 3-digit SIC Herfindahl Index (HERF) and three dummy variables based on 4 and 8 firm concentration ratios representing high (H), medium (M) and low (L) concentration industries. The correlation matrix for these measures is presented in the following table.

Correlation Matrix: Concentration Measures

	H	M	L	HERF
H	1.000	−.629	−.374	.791
M		1.000	−.485	−.346
L			1.000	−.477
HERF				1.000

It can be seen that the two sets of measures are related, and that the dummy variables themselves are related. It was therefore decided to concentrate on HERF as the measure of industrial concentration, since this is a simpler measure to process statistically, and its use avoids possible multicollinearity. Experimentation indicated that none of the results of this study would change if the dummy variables were employed.

For the moment, however, we will use both sets of variables to examine the concentration levels of the control groups used in this study. These are found in Table II-5.

This table reveals that of the 246 (32.7%) firms classified as H, CAN and OF firms are over-represented, the latter more than the former, while U.S. firms are under-represented. For example, U.S. firms represent 48.3% of the sample firms, but only 44.1% of the H firms. Furthermore, only 29.8% of U.S. firms were classified as H. Conversely, U.S. firms are over-represented in the L category, while Canadian and OF firms are under-represented, the latter more than the former. The M category is mixed. The Herfindahl Index presents the same information: OF firms are represented in the most concentrated industries, and U.S. firms in the least concentrated.

The chi-squared statistic indicates that the differences in representation by control group are not significant. The t-test applied to the HERF means indicates that OF firms' HERF is nearly (12% level) significantly higher than the other two, which are not significantly different from each other.

TABLE II-5

Concentration Levels by Control Group

	U.S.	OF	CAN	TOTAL
H n	108	40	97	245
% H	44.1	16.3	39.6	32.7
% country	29.8	40.8	33.4	
M n	168	39	130	337
% M	49.9	11.6	38.6	44.9
% country	46.4	39.8	44.8	
L n	86	19	63	168
% L	51.2	11.3	37.5	22.4
% country	23.8	19.4	21.7	
TOTAL n	362	98	290	
%	48.3	13.1	38.7	
HERF (mean)	.105	.120	.108	.108

In spite of the absence of a statistically significant relation, this result is somewhat surprising in light of the theory of the multinational firm which suggests that multinationals tend to be oligopolists who transfer their industrial structure abroad. It does, however, confirm a similar result produced by Rosenbluth (1970). It should be recalled that we are dealing only with a sample of the largest firms, the excluded small firms being mostly Canadian-controlled, and in less concentrated industries.[9]

Table II-6 extends the analysis to size groups. It is seen that there is a tendency for larger firms to be found in more concentrated industries. This tendency exists for all control groups, with only minor deviations. One of these is found in the CAN group where the very largest firms are not found in the most concentrated industries. This results from the fact that the largest Canadian firms in the sample are in the wood industries where concentration is not as high as in other industries where large firms are found, such as petroleum.

TABLE II-6

Size and Concentration by Control Group

(Herfindahl Index)

Size Class (Assets) (000,000)	U.S.	OF	CAN	TOTAL
1. <5	.100	.113	.079	.092
2. 5-10	.080	.098	.087	.085
3. 10-20	.101	.087	.116	.105
4. 20-40	.130	.120	.135	.130
5. 40-80	.133	.158	.135	.140
6. 80-160	.113	.126	.157	.133
7. >160	.178	.291	.104	.163
TOTAL	.105	.120	.108	.108

The simple correlation coefficients between size (assets) and log size (assets) and the Herfindahl Index confirms the above result.

Simple Correlation Coefficients

	Size-Herf	Log Size-Herf
U.S.	.199*	.249*
OF	.230*	.315*
CAN	.090*	.187*
TOTAL	.168*	.236*

*significant at 5%

The coefficients are all significant albeit small, thus confirming that there is some tendency for large firms to be found in the most concentrated industries. This relationship is weakest in the Canadian case, particularly when absolute size is used.

II-5 Summary and Conclusions

The sample consists of 750 of Canada's largest manufacturing firms over the period 1968-1972. Data for each firm exists for each of the five sample years. Firms are classified as Canadian-controlled, U.S.-controlled, or Other Foreign-controlled.

An analysis of the sample reveals that foreign-controlled firms (either U.S. or Other Foreign) are on average slightly larger than Canadian-controlled firms when size is measured by assets. However, the difference is not statistically significant and is explained by the concentration of foreign-controlled firms in industries where average firm size is large (petroleum, in particular). When size is measured by sales, U.S.-controlled firms are found to be larger than either Canadian or Other Foreign firms, and this difference is statistically significant.

U.S.-controlled firms do not tend to cluster in high-concentration industries, but Other Foreign firms do. Large firms are found in more concentrated industries, although this tendency is not strong and differs by control group. Large Canadian-controlled firms are less likely to be found in a highly concentrated industry than are large foreign-controlled firms.

Notes

1. See the discussion of the classification procedure in the introduction to the various CALURA reports.

2. *Industrial Organization and Concentration in the Manufacturing, Mining and Logging Industries*, Ottawa, May 1973 (catalogue number 31-514 occasional).

3. See the Appendix to this chapter for a list of the 3-digit industries which comprise each of the 13 2-digit industries.

4. A statistical analysis of merging firms is provided by R. Hinchcliff and D. Shapiro, *Take-Overs in Canada, 1968-1972*, mimeo, Statistics Canada, 1976.

5. This discussion on total Canadian industries is based on ratios computed by *The Financial Post Computer Services*, Toronto, March 1975.

6. Selected financial ratios by industry may be found in: Statistics Canada, *Industrial Corporations Financial Statistics* (Cat. No. 61-003), annual.

7. See U.S. Government, *Economic Report of the President*, Washington, Feb. 1974, pp. 336-340; U.S. Internal Revenue Service, Department of the Treasury, *Corporation Income Tax Returns*, Washington, Jan. 1974; Troy, Leo, *Almanac of Business and Industrial Financial Ratios*, Prentice-Hall, 1972.

8. To determine whether an observed difference was significant, an analysis of variance was performed on the group means. See the notes at the bottom of Table II-3.

9. This result is also surprising because it will be shown in Chapter IV that U.S. firms are less likely to experience losses. Yet, they are also underrepresented in high concentration industries where greater stability might be thought to exist.

Appendix to Chapter II: Master Variable List

The following financial variables are available for each year of 1968-1972.

I. Assets

1. accounts receivable
2. inventories (gross)
3. due from affiliates (short-term)
4. total current assets
5. total depreciable assets (buildings and equipment)
6. accumulated depreciation
7. net fixed assets (5-6)
8. total fixed assets
9. investments in affiliates
10. due from affiliates (long-term)
11. other assets
12. total other assets
13. total assets

II. Liabilities

14. accounts payable
15. due to affiliates (short-term)
16. total current liabilities
17. due to affiliates (long-term)
18. net long-term debt
19. total non-current liabilities

III. Equity

20. preferred shares
21. total equity

IV. Deductions

22. gross profit (book)
23. reported cost of sales
24. wages and salaries in cost of sales
25. repairs and maintenance in cost of sales
26. depreciation in cost of sales
27. depletion in cost of sales
28. materials cost (residual = 23-24-25-26-27)
29. total salaries and wages
30. bond interest
31. mortgage interest
32. other interest
33. royalties
34. total depreciation
35. total depletion
36. taxes paid
37. management and administration fees
38. total deductions

V. Revenue

39. sales-products
40. total revenue

VI. Profits

41. opening balance
42. net profit (loss)
43. cash dividends paid
44. stock dividends paid
45. other charges/credits
46. closing balance = retained earnings

VII. Capital Expenditures

47. land
48. depletable assets
49. buildings
50. equipment

VIII. Other Variables

51. Country of Control = U.S., Canada, Other Foreign
52. Non-resident Ownership Radio (NRO)
53. 3-digit SIC
54. High Concentration (H)

55. Medium Concentration (M)
56. Low Concentration (L)
57. Herfindahl Index (HERF)
58. Producers Good (P)
59. Consumers Convenience Good (C)
60. Consumers Non-Convenience Good (N)
61. Food and Beverages (non alcoholic) (SIC = 101, 103, 105, 107, 111, 112, 123, 124, 125, 128, 129, 131, 133, 135, 139, 141)
62. Leather, Clothing, Textiles (SIC = 172, 174, 183, 197, 201, 212, 213, 214, 216, 219, 229, 231, 239, 243, 248)
63. Wood Products (SIC = 251-259)
64. Pulp and Paper (SIC = 271-274)
65. Primary Metals (SIC = 291-298)
66. Metal Fabricating (SIC = 301-309)
67. Machinery (SIC = 311, 315, 316, 318)
68. Transportation Equipment (SIC = 321-329)
69. Electrical Products (SIC = 331-339, 381-385)
70. Non-Metallic Minerals (SIC = 341, 345, 349, 351, 354-357)
71. Petroleum and Coal (SIC = 365, 369)
72. Chemical (SIC = 371-379)
73. Miscellaneous (SIC = 143-147, 151, 153, 161, 163, 169, 261, 264, 266, 286-289, 393, 397, 399)

III

FINANCIAL STRUCTURE

III-1 Introduction

The purpose of this chapter is to compare the financial structures of Canadian-, U.S.-, and Other Foreign-controlled firms in Canada. It has already been pointed out that there are strong theoretical reasons to believe that differences in financial structure exist, and that these differences are caused by the unique behaviour of MNCs and their subsidiaries. Thus, the analysis of financial structures is relevant to both the evolving study of MNCs and their impact on the Canadian economy.

Financial structure will be defined by a series of financial ratios, and the analysis will focus on inter-group differences (if any) in these ratios. Statistical tests will be performed in order to ascertain whether these differences are significant. This type of procedure, whereby financial ratios for pre-defined, fixed categories (in this case country of control) are compared amongst groups, or for a single group over time, is common among financial analysts and business economists. The purpose of such an analysis is therefore to uncover differences in financial ratios amongst groups. When (and if) differences are encountered the analyst might attempt to explain them by considering further explanatory variables, or by inference from economic theory. For the purposes of this study, the theory of the MNC will serve as a guide to the explanation of financial differences.

There are many financial ratios which can be constructed from a balance sheet and, in addition, a single concept may be measured in a number of ways, thus resulting in an unmanageable number of potential ratios. As a consequence, some researchers have attempted to develop "empirically based classifications (taxonomies) of financial ratios" (Johnson, 1978, p. 207). For the purposes of this study, financial ratios were chosen to conform to the theoretical considerations of Chapter I and to facilitate comparisons with the existing literature, particularly Pattison (1978). The ratios were then grouped into categories. These categories are not empirically based, but were chosen to reflect common usage as well as empirically-derived categories.[1] The financial ratios are defined in Section III-2.

Profitability is an important element in a firm's financial structure, and is normally included in any financial analysis. Profitability is also crucial to the study of firm performance, particularly in the area of industrial economics, and will therefore be accorded a separate analysis in Chapters IV and V.

The subject matter considered in this chapter is very similar to that found in Chapter III of Pattison's above-cited study. In that chapter Pattison analysed financial ratios for foreign- and Canadian-controlled firms. Because his data were aggregated, it was not possible for him to perform statistical tests on group means. Because this study uses non-aggregated data, statistical testing of inter-group means is possible, and such is the purpose of Section III-3. The analysis is extended in Section III-4 to account for the effects of industry, size, and growth on inter-firm differences in financial structure. Section III-5 summarizes the results of these tests, compares them with Pattison's results and draws conclusions regarding the nature of foreign-controlled firms in Canada.

III-2 Financial Variables: Definitions

The purpose of this section is to define and explain the financial ratios to be employed in the comparative financial analysis of foreign-and Canadian-controlled firms. This information is summarized in Table III-1.

The first group of variables measures the capital intensity and/or capital efficiency of the firm. Because there is no single definition of capital intensity when financial variables are used, and because there is some ambiguity surrounding some of these variables, several measures have been employed.[2] KIT is the ratio of assets to sales, and is often employed as a proxy for the physical capital-output ratio. Nevertheless, it is equally likely that this variable measures the

TABLE III-1

Financial Variables

Group	Variable	Symbol	Calculation*
Capital Intensiveness/	Capital Turnover	KIT	13/39
Capital Efficiency	Fixed Asset Turnover	FATO	39/8
	Labour Intensiveness (Total)	ULT	29/38
	Labour Intensiveness (Production)	ULP	24/38
Capital Structure	Current Assets	CATA	4/13
(% of Total Assets)	Receivables	RCTA	1/13
	Inventories	INVTA	4/13
	Fixed Assets	FATA	8/13
	Other Assets	OATA	12/13
	Investment in Affiliates	IATA	9/13
Leverage	Non-Current Liabilities	LEV	19/13
(% of Total Assets)	Retained Earnings	RETA	46/13
	Net Long-Term Debt	LEVT	18/13
Payout	Payout	APO	43/42
Liquidity	Current Ratio	LIQ	4/16
	Quick Ratio	QCK	(4-2)/13
	Working Capital	WKTA	(4-16)/13
	Current Asset Turnover	CATO	39/2
	Inventory Turnover	INVTO	39/4

* Numbers refer to those in the Appendix to Chapter II.

efficiency of capital usage, i.e., the dollar assets required to generate a dollar of sales. In this event, a lower value of KIT would imply greater efficiency in capital usage rather than lower capital intensity. A similar measure is FATO, the fixed asset turnover ratio, which excludes current and other assets, and therefore more closely approximates the use of physical capital. The evidence presented in Chapter II suggests that U.S. firms may be more efficient in utilizing their capital (assets), and KIT and FATO might capture this effect rather than capital intensity. In an attempt to further separate these effects, other measures of capital intensity were calculated. ULP and ULT are labour-intensity measures, labour-intensity being simply the inverse of capital intensity. The two measures differ only in the numerator. ULP comprises wages and salaries paid to production workers, while ULT comprises all wages and salaries, including those paid to administrative and office workers.

The capital structure group simply decomposes the assets of the firm into constituent parts: current (CATA), fixed (FATA), and other assets (OATA). The current asset component is further broken down to account for receivables (RCTA) and inventories (INVTA), factors which were identified in Chapter I as being potential sources of difference between foreign- and domestic-controlled firms. It was suggested that foreign-controlled firms might rely more on receivables as a method of financing transactions, and that they might be more inventory intensive. In addition, the other assets component has been decomposed to account for investments in affiliated companies (IATA). The relevance of this variable was also pointed out in Chapter I where it was suggested that Canadian-controlled firms may be more willing to diversify their investment portfolios in Canada, while foreign-controlled firms might simply remit such funds to the parent.

Leverage ratios, found in the next group, measure the extent to which firms finance themselves through debt, as opposed to using internally generated funds (retained earnings) or new issues. The most commonly used leverage ratio is the debt-equity ratio. For the purposes of this study, the debt-equity ratio was deemed inadequate because it was felt that equity did not represent the value of the firm to its owners in the case of subsidiaries of foreign firms, which also supplied considerable debt capital, both long- and short-term, to the affiliate.[3] This is particularly true in the case of affiliates which are owned 100% by their parent. A further complication arises when equity is employed, and it is caused by the tendency of MNCs to undercapitalize their subsidiaries in some cases. This produces a bias when equity-based ratios are compared. As a consequence, the leverage measures employed here are all measured using assets in the denominator. LEV represents the extent to which the firm relies on debt from all sources, including its affiliates, expressed as a proportion of total assets. LEVT is the same as LEV, save that it nets out funds which are borrowed from affiliated companies. This is important when considering foreign-controlled firms, since they may borrow relatively heavily from affiliated firms, including their parents. RETA represents the extent to which retained funds are used, and is actually the mirror image of LEV. The analysis in Chapter I leads to the expectation that foreign-controlled firms in Canada (although not necessarily elsewhere) will be relatively less highly levered.

The payout ratio, here defined as cash dividends per dollar of profit, is self-explanatory and is included to account for the possibility that foreign-controlled firms pay out dividends at a higher rate as a method of repatriating funds.

The final group comprises variables related to the liquidity position of the firm, i.e., its ability to meet current obligations. Liquidity has both a transactions component (the ability to meet current payments) and a precautionary component (liquid assets accumulated to meet unforseen expenses). There are several commonly used liquidity ratios. LIQ, called the current ratio, is the ratio of current assets to current liabilities. The quick ratio, QCK, is identical to LIQ, save that inventories are netted out of the numerator on the grounds that inventories are less liquid than cash or short-term securities. WKTA takes working capital (current assets less current liabilities) as a percentage of total assets. Included in the liquidity group are two ratios which do not precisely measure liquidity, but rather are concerned with the efficiency with which current assets are employed. These are the current asset and inventory turnover ratios. More efficient use of current assets may allow the firm to be relatively less liquid, and these variables are included to control for this possibility. Again, liquidity has been identified as a financial group in which foreign-controlled firms have been found to differ from Canadian-controlled firms.

We are now in a position to analyse the computed values of these variables by control group.

III-3 Financial Structure: Univariate Analysis

Table III-2 presents an analysis of variance of the calculated ratios, averaged over the five-year period, by country of control. Before considering this table, a *caveat* is in order. These ratios are calculated from individual firm data with each firm representing a single, unweighted observation. Thus, all firms, both large and small, have equal weight in the average. This, of course, is the normal procedure for analysing individual firm behaviour. However, published data are often weighted averages, and the reader is therefore cautioned against comparing the ratios found in Table III-2 with published ratios (such as those found in the CALURA reports).[4]

The analysis of variance seeks to ascertain whether there are significant differences among the (averaged) means of the three control groups (Canada, U.S., Other Foreign). When such differences are found, they are indicated by the superscripts 1, 2 or 3. Superscript 1 indicates that the variable in question is significantly different (at the 5% level) from the corresponding U.S variable; 2 indicates that it is different from the corresponding Other Foreign variable; and 3 indicates that it is different from the corresponding Canadian variable.[5]

TABLE III-2

ANALYSIS OF VARIANCE OF AVERAGED FINANCIAL VARIABLES,

BY COUNTRY OF CONTROL*

CAPITAL INTENSIVENESS/CAPITAL EFFICIENCY

		KIT	FATO	ULT	ULP
U.S.	M	$1.10^{1,\,3}$	6.14	$.22^{2,\,3}$	.17
	(S)	(.99)	(6.14)	(.09)	(.09)
OTHER	M	1.60^{1}	5.65	$.21^{1,\,3}$	$.16^{3}$
FOREIGN	(S)	(1.76)	(8.46)	(.08)	(.08)
CANADA	M	1.45^{1}	5.52	$.24^{1,\,2}$	$.18^{2}$
	(S)	(2.22)	(6.66)	(.10)	(.09)
TOTAL	M	1.29	5.85	.23	.18
	(S)	(1.40)	(8.39)	(.10)	(.09)

CAPITAL STRUCTURE

		CATA	RCTA	INVTA	FATA	IATA	OATA
U.S.	M	$.57^{2,\,3}$	$.18^{2,\,3}$	$.15^{2,\,3}$	$.34^{2}$	$.04^{2,\,3}$	$.09^{2,\,3}$
	(S)	(.20)	(.11)	(.10)	(.18)	(.09)	(.12)
OTHER	M	$.49^{1}$	$.15^{1}$	$.09^{1}$	$.39^{1,\,3}$	$.06^{1}$	$.12^{1,\,3}$
FOREIGN	(S)	(.22)	(.10)	(.08)	(.21)	(.11)	(.16)
CANADA	M	$.50^{1}$	$.16^{1}$	$.10^{1}$	$.34^{2}$	$.08^{1}$	$.16^{1,\,2}$
	(S)	(.21)	(.11)	(.07)	(.19)	(.12)	(.18)
TOTAL	M	.53	.17	.12	.35	.06	.12
	(S)	(.21)	(.11)	(.09)	(.19)	(.15)	(.16)

PAYOUT

		APO
U.S.	M	−.35
	(S)	(.88)
OTHER	M	−.17
FOREIGN	(S)	(1.18)
CANADA	M	−.47
	(S)	(7.82)
TOTAL	M	−.37
	(S)	(4.91)

LEVERAGE

		LEV	RETA	LEVT
U.S.	M	$.17^{2,\,3}$	$.41^{2,\,3}$	$.05^{2,\,3}$
	(S)	(.19)	(.25)	(.11)

III—FINANCIAL STRUCTURE 39

TABLE III-2 (Cont'd.)

OTHER	M	.27[1]	.16[1,3]	.15[1,3]
FOREIGN	(S)	(.24)	(.24)	(.18)
CANADA	M	.24[1]	.21[1,2]	.12[1,2]
	(S)	(.21)	(.28)	(.12)
TOTAL	M	.21	.32	.09
	(S)	(.21)	(.28)	(.13)

LIQUIDITY

		LIQ	QCK	NKTA	INVTO	CATO
U.S.	M	2.94[2,3]	1.58[2]	.29[2,3]	6.18[3]	2.74
	(S)	(2.19)	(1.53)	(.19)	(5.25)	(2.90)
OTHER	M	2.07[1,3]	1.05[1,3]	.19[1]	6.67	2.45[3]
FOREIGN	(S)	(1.28)	(.72)	(.17)	(6.50)	(1.32)
CANADA	M	2.41[1,2]	1.66[2]	.18[1]	7.45[1]	2.83[2]
	(S)	(2.46)	(4.61)	(.18)	(7.26)	(2.00)
TOTAL	M	2.62	1.54	.23	6.74	2.71
	(S)	(2.23)	(3.07)	(.19)	(6.47)	(2.21)

*Notes

Variables are averaged over 1968-1972
M = mean
S = standard deviation
1 = significantly different from U.S. (at 5%, two-tailed test)
2 = significantly different from Other Foreign (at 5%, two-tailed test)
3 = significantly different from Canada (at 5%, two-tailed test)

This type of analysis is useful for discerning differences in the means, but it cannot isolate the source of the differences since all firms in each control group are being compared, regardless of industry or firm size. A consideration of these factors will be delayed until the next section.

Since most of the ratios showed no particular cyclical trend, the major emphasis is placed on the averages. Certain ratios, however, not only exhibited cyclical tendencies, but these differed among the control groups. Such ratios are presented in Table III-3.

Table III-2 reveals that there are significant differences among the control groups. As expected, U.S.-controlled firms have the lowest total asset turnover ratio (KIT), and it is significantly lower than that for either Canadian- or Other Foreign-controlled firms (which are not significantly different from each other). This does not necessarily imply that U.S. firms are less capital intensive, but is more likely to reflect the efficiency with which they utilize their capital stock. This latter interpretation cannot be extended to fixed assets turnover

(FATO), where no significant differences exist among the control groups. When labour costs are examined, it can be seen that Other Foreign firms have the lowest ratio, followed by U.S.- and Canadian-controlled firms. When only production labour is considered, the differences are not significant and only become so when overhead labour is included.[6]

Table III-2 indicates that there are significant differences among the groups in terms of capital structure. In general, U.S. firms are "top heavy" and Canadian firms are "bottom heavy", i.e., U.S.-controlled firms have a higher percentage of their assets in liquid (current) form (CATA), while Canadian-controlled firms have a higher percentage in Other Assets (OATA), particularly investments in affiliates (IATA). There is virtually no difference in the percentage of fixed assets employed by the two groups. The current asset intensity of U.S.-controlled firms is caused by their relatively higher inventory and receivables percentages (INVTA and RCTA). Furthermore, LIQ and WKTA, two liquidity measures, are higher for U.S.-controlled firms. But when inventories are netted out (QCK), the relationship ceases to be significant; indeed, Canadian-controlled firms tend to be more liquid according to this measure, although the difference is not significant. The high standard deviation leaves this result in some doubt. It appears that the high U.S. liquidity is accounted for by inventories and receivables. The latter is not surprising in view of the likelihood that U.S. firms utilize receivables as a means of extending credit, and perhaps remitting funds, to the parent. The inventory result might be considered unexpected, in light of the view that subsidiaries of large, U.S. firms should be able to achieve economies of scale in inventory management. Indeed, Table III-2 indicates that U.S.-controlled firms are significantly less efficient in turning over their inventory (see INVTO). It will be recalled, however, that Robbins and Stobaugh (1974) did hypothesize such an outcome. It should be noted that Other Foreign-controlled firms are not more inventory intensive that Canadian-controlled firms, nor are they less efficient in turning over their inventories.

In addition, Other Foreign firms appear to be more fixed-asset intensive and less liquid than the others. This could well be caused by their relative youth in Canada. It is possible that some of the newer non-American firms, particularly those which are Japanese-controlled, have not yet had time to establish a solid short-term position because of long-term capital commitments, i.e., they are engaged in large, new capital projects relative to older firms. This might explain their high fixed-asset intensity.

The payout ratios provide little information. Canadian-controlled firms have the highest payout rates, on average, and Other Foreign-controlled firms the lowest. There are no significant differences among the groups, but the numbers must be viewed with some caution owing to the high standard deviations.

Lastly, we consider the relative leverage of the sample firms. From Table III-2 it is apparent that American firms are the least highly levered, and rely the most on retained earnings. Other Foreign firms rely most heavily on debt, with Canadian-controlled firms in-between. The differences are highly significant. Furthermore, what borrowing U.S.-controlled firms do engage in, is from affiliated companies. The ratio of LEVT (mostly bank debt) to LEV (total debt) is .32 for U.S.-controlled firms, .56 for Other Foreign-controlled firms, and .47 for Canadian-controlled firms. Thus U.S.-controlled firms rely on affiliated companies for about two-thirds of their debt, as opposed to both Canadian- and Other Foreign-controlled firms for which the fraction is about one-half. Given the known proclivity of U.S. firms to prefer retained earnings to debt, this result suggests that national norms are an important factor in U.S.-subsidiary financial behaviour.

The information contained in Table III-3 indicates that U.S.-controlled firms not only prefer retentions to debt, but that this tendency grew over the sample period. While Canadian-controlled firms came to rely more on debt and less on retained earnings, the reverse was true for both U.S.- and Other Foreign-controlled firms. U.S.-controlled firms also tended to become steadily more liquid over the period, and this increase in liquidity was caused by both increases in inventory accumulation and increases in other current assets. The position of Canadian-controlled firms tended to vary over the period, with little change in LIQ, but with an improvement in QCK.[7] Over-all, the liquidity position of Other Foreign firms deteriorated over the period.

The general conclusion which emerges from this section is that there are indeed differences in the financial structures of the control groups, particularly where leverage and liquidity are concerned. Furthermore, there are differences between U.S.- and Other Foreign-controlled firms, leading to the conclusion that foreign-controlled firms are not similar in some respects, and therefore policies regarding foreign ownership should not treat the foreign-owned sector of the economy as a bloc.

Specifically, it has been found that U.S.-controlled firms are more efficient in their total capital usage, but this result does not hold when assets are broken down into fixed and current components. The over-all efficiency of U.S.-controlled firms may be partly attributed to the fact that such firms devote a relatively low percentage of their assets to investments in affiliates and other forms of assets cre-

TABLE III-3

SELECTED FINANCIAL RATIOS, ANNUAL VALUES BY COUNTRY OF CONTROL*

VARIABLE	COUNTRY OF CONTROL	1968 M	1969 M	1970 M	1971 M	1972 M
LEV	U.S.	$.174^{2,3}$	$.166^{2,3}$	$.169^{2,3}$	$.157^{2,3}$	$.158^{2,3}$
	O.F.	$.282^{1,3}$	$.276^{3}$	$.269^{1}$	$.263^{1}$	$.244^{1}$
	CAN.	$.240^{1,2}$	$.238^{1,2}$	$.238^{1}$	$.251^{1}$	$.248^{1}$
	TOTAL	.214	.208	.209	.207	.204
RETA	U.S.	$.384^{2,3}$	$.399^{2,3}$	$.406^{2,3}$	$.425^{2,3}$	$.423^{2,3}$
	O.F.	$.146^{1,3}$	$.146^{1,3}$	$.142^{1,3}$	$.162^{1,3}$	$.185^{1,3}$
	CAN.	$.265^{1,2}$	$.263^{1,2}$	$.261^{1,2}$	$.258^{1,2}$	$.254^{1,2}$
	TOTAL	.307	.314	.315	.362	.318
LEVT	U.S.	$.059^{2,3}$	$.054^{2,3}$	$.053^{2,3}$	$.049^{2,3}$	$.046^{2,3}$
	O.F.	$.152^{1,3}$	$.148^{1,3}$	$.157^{1,3}$	$.151^{1,3}$	$.136^{1,3}$
	CAN.	$.118^{1,2}$	$.114^{1,2}$	$.118^{1,2}$	$.111^{1,2}$	$.113^{1,2}$
	TOTAL	.094	.090	.092	.086	.084
LIQ	U.S.	$2.761^{2,3}$	$2.792^{2,3}$	$2.907^{2,3}$	$2.932^{2,3}$	$3.034^{2,3}$
	O.F.	2.209^{1}	2.001^{1}	2.040^{1}	$2.023^{1,3}$	2.086^{1}
	CAN.	2.318^{1}	2.186^{1}	2.353^{1}	$2.467^{1,2}$	2.355^{1}
	TOTAL	2.519	2.453	2.580	2.633	2.654
WKTA	U.S.	$.272^{2,3}$	$.274^{2,3}$	$.280^{2,3}$	$.296^{2,3}$	$.308^{2,3}$
	O.F.	$.194^{1}$	$.187^{1}$	$.182^{1}$	$.190^{1}$	$.187^{1}$
	CAN.	$.188^{1}$	$.179^{1}$	$.172^{1}$	$.180^{1}$	$.179^{1}$
	TOTAL	.229	.226	.225	.243	.243
QCK	U.S.	1.512^{2}	1.441^{2}	1.538^{2}	1.661^{2}	1.750^{2}
	O.F.	1.151^{1}	$1.008^{1,3}$	$1.014^{1,3}$	$1.017^{1,3}$	$1.091^{1,3}$
	CAN.	1.453	1.322^{2}	1.812^{2}	1.734^{2}	2.001^{2}
	TOTAL	1.442	1.330	1.577	1.607	1.768

* **Notes:** See Table III-2.

ation. While no differences in labour-intensity could be found among the groups when only production labour was considered, it was found that Other Foreign- and Canadian-controlled firms tended to devote a greater percentage of costs to the employment of overhead labour. In the case of U.S.-controlled firms, one might attribute this to the truncation of the firm whereby certain activities are reserved for the parent, particularly in the areas of financial and investment planning, product development, and research and development. These are all areas where overhead labour is important. One would also expect that Other Foreign firms would exhibit the same features, but this is not the case.

U.S.-controlled firms appear to be more liquid, but this is caused by their relative inventory and receivables intensiveness, while Other Foreign-controlled firms are highly illiquid by any measure.

U.S.-controlled firms are the least levered firms, while Other Foreign-controlled firms are the most levered. It remains the purpose of the next section to ascertain whether these differences persist when industry and other factors are accounted for.

III-4 Financial Structure: Regression Analysis

It is possible that financial differences, attributed in the previous section to country of control, may in fact be caused by other factors, particularly the industry composition of the sample. Not only may different industries follow different financial norms, but the nature of the product and the technology required to produce it may result in financial differences among firms. In addition to industry, there are other factors which may affect a firm's financial structure, such as firm size and firm growth.[8] In order to correctly assess the role that country of control plays in explaining inter-firm differences in financial structure, these factors must be accounted for.

The general method employed in this section is the regression of the relevant financial ratio on independent variables representing the firm's industry, its country of control, its size, and its rate of growth.[9] Industry is represented by the 13 industry dummy variables described in Chapter II, firm size is measured in assets, and firm growth is represented by the average annual rate of growth of sales.[10]

This procedure does have its drawbacks. The estimated equations are not derived from an economic or financial model designed to explain interfirm differences in each financial variable.[11] As a consequence, in any given equation there are likely to be omitted variables, thus raising the possibility that included variables are reflecting other factors. In addition, the results of this procedure cannot always be interpreted unambiguously. For example, if inter-firm differences in a variable are attributed to industry factors rather than country of control, but if the industry happens to be highly foreign-owned, then it is not clear whether foreign ownership can be discounted as an explanatory factor.

We now turn to the regression results presented in Table III-4. In general, it was found that the regression equations did not significantly alter the conclusions presented in the previous section. Therefore, only selected regression equations are presented.[12] As in the regression equations presented to analyse firm size in Chapter II, the dummy variables representing Miscellaneous Manufacturing industries and Other Foreign firms are omitted from the equations. When a coefficient is indicated as being significant, one should in-

TABLE III-4

FINANCIAL VARIABLES: SELECTED REGRESSION RESULTS

DEPENDENT VARIABLE

INDEPENDENT VARIABLE	(1) KIT	(2) ULP	(3) FATA	(4) CATA	(5) RCTA	(6) IATA
Food and Beverages	−.60* (.18)	−.04* (.01)	.09* (.03)	−.11* (.03)	−.02 (.02)	.02 (.02)
Leather, Clothing, Textiles	−.42* (.20)	.07* (.01)	−.01 (.03)	.04 (.03)	.04* (.02)	−.00 (.03)
Wood	−.14 (.23)	.04* (.02)	.11* (.03)	−.10* (.03)	−.04* (.02)	−.00 (.02)
Pulp and Paper	.42* (.19)	.04* (.01)	.20* (.03)	−.18* (.03)	−.05* (.02)	−.00 (.02)
Primary Metals	−.30 (.22)	.03* (.01)	.13* (.03)	−.10* (.03)	.02 (.02)	−.02 (.03)
Metal Fabricating	.04 (.19)	.05* (.01)	−.02 (.03)	.04 (.03)	.05* (.02)	−.01 (.02)
Machinery	−.35** (.20)	.02* (.01)	−.08* (.03)	.15* (.03)	.08* (.02)	−.02 (.02)
Transportation Equipment	−.42* (.19)	.05* (.01)	−.02 (.03)	.05** (.03)	.03* (.01)	−.01 (.02)
Electrical	−.41* (.19)	.02* (.01)	−.06* (.03)	.09* (.03)	.07* (.02)	.00 (.02)
Non-Metallic Minerals	.17 (.25)	.06* (.02)	.21* (.04)	−.20* (.04)	−.02 (.02)	.02 (.02)
Petroleum	.47 (.35)	−.11* (.02)	.31* (.05)	−.27* (.05)	−.04 (.03)	−.04 (.03)
Chemicals	−.28 (.19)	.03* (.01)	.06* (.03)	−.05** (.03)	.03* (.01)	.01 (.02)
U.S.	−.34* (.13)	.02** (.01)	.00 (.02)	.03** (.02)	.01 (.01)	−.02* (.01)
CANADA	−.14 (.14)	.02 (.02)	−.02 (.02)	−.01 (.02)	.01 (.01)	.01 (.01)
Size (assets)²	.00 (.00)	.00 (.00)	.00 (.00)	−.00* (.00)	−.00* (.00)	.00* (.00)
Growth (sales)	.29 (.18)		.08* (.03)			
constant	1.50	.14	.30	.56	.15	.06
R̄²	.10	.19	.28	.32	.18	.05

n = 750

TABLE III-4(Cont'd)

DEPENDENT VARIABLE

INDEPENDENT VARIABLE	(7) INVTO	(8) CATO	(9) LEV	(10) LEVT	(11) LIQ	(12) QCK
Food and Beverages	8.40*(1.05)	2.44*(.54)	.04 (.03)	.03 (.02)	—1.48* (.67)	— .50(.47)
Leather, Clothing, Textiles	.16 (1.17)	— .03 (.60)	.00 (.03)	.03 (.02)	.02 (.74)	.62(.52)
Wood	1.74 (.134)	.47 (.69)	.11* (.04)	.06* (.02)	.06 (.85)	.79(.60)
Pulp and Paper	2.10*(1.11)	.71*(.35)	.15* (.03)	.10* (.02)	.74 (.70)	— .01(.49)
Primary Metals	1.25 (1.32)	.48 (.68)	.09* (.04)	.04* (.02)	.80 (.83)	— .09(.58)
Metal Fabricating	.68 (1.10)	— .19 (.59)	—.01 (.03)	.00 (.02)	.94 (.70)	— .09(.49)
Machinery	— .94 (1.20)	— .36 (.62)	—.03 (.03)	—.01 (.02)	.74 (.76)	.09(.49)
Transportation Equipment	1.10 (1.34)	.41 (.59)	—.02 (.03)	.00 (.02)	—1.61* (.70)	— .03(.53)
Electrical	.14 (1.15)	— .03 (.59)	—.01 (.03)	.01 (.02)	—1.02 (.73)	.53(.51)
Non-Metallic Minerals	2.11 (1.47)	.60 (.76)	.07**(.04)	.08* (.03)	.86 (.94)	.21(.51)
Petroleum	9.38*(2.05)	6.66*(.98)	.14 (.58)	.04 (.03)	—1.10 (1.20)	.27(.66)
Chemicals	1.61 (1.15)	.24 (.60)	.04 (.03)	.04* (.02)	— .37 (.73)	.11(.85)
U.S.	— .41 (.80)	.49 (.41)	—.08* (.02)	.08* (.01)	1.21* (.51)	.47(.51)
Canada	.60 (.83)	.51 (.43)	—.01 (.02)	—.03**(.02)	.79**(.50)	.51(.36)
Size (Assets)	— .00 (.00)	— .00*(.00)	.00 (.00)	.00* (.00)	.00 (.00)	.55(.37)
Growth (Sales)	—5.87*(1.11)	—4.35*(.55)	.06* (.03)	.10* (.02)		.00(.00)
Constant	5.32	1.80	.21	.10	2.71	1.10
R̄²	.17	.19	.13	.19	.13	.02

Notes: 1. Figures in parentheses are standard errors.

   * = significant at 5%, two-tailed test

   ** = significant at 10%, two-tailed test

2. Significance levels are calculated from figures calculated to 6 decimals. When significant, the size term took a value of .000001 and may be read as such.

terpret this in relation to the reference group which is defined by the omitted dummy variables.

Equation (1) confirms that U.S.-controlled firms are more efficient in their total capital usage, after correction for industry. For example, the capital-sales ratio of a firm in the pulp and paper industry is .42 points higher than the reference firm. However, if the firm is U.S.-controlled, its ratio falls by .34 points. Thus, a U.S.-controlled pulp and paper firm will, on average, have a lower KIT than either a Canadian- or Other Foreign-controlled firm. When production labour costs are examined in equation (2), it is seen that the coefficients for the U.S. and Canada dummy variables are exactly equal, although the Canadian coefficient is not quite significant at 10%, while the U.S. coefficient is barely significant at that level, when unrounded figures are used to calculate significance levels. Differences in labour costs appear to be attributable to industry.[13]

Equations (3) to (6) relate to the capital structure of the firm. These equations confirm that there are no differences amongst the control groups in the percentage of assets which are fixed. The univariate analysis suggested that Other Foreign firms were more fixed asset intensive, but this appears to be explained by their investments in petroleum and pulp and paper industries. As before, U.S.-controlled firms are found to be more current asset intensive (although the U.S. coefficient is significant at only the 10% level), while there is no difference between Canadian and Other Foreign firms. However, whereas the univariate analysis suggested that U.S. firms were more receivables intensive, the regression analysis fails to confirm this. Although the U.S. coefficient is not significant, a problem of interpretation arises because the largest positive (and significant) coefficients are those associated with the Machinery and Non-Metallic Minerals industries, both of which are highly foreign-owned. Regression analysis indicates that U.S.-controlled firms are more inventory intensive, regardless of industry, a point which will be considered again momentarily. Lastly, it is confirmed that U.S.-controlled firms invest less in affiliated firms than either Canadian or Other Foreign firms.

When inventory and current asset turnover ratios are considered in equations (7) and (8), it is found that no differences among the control groups emerge, a result which is not quite consistent with the univariate analysis.[14] The univariate analysis suggested that Canadian firms were more efficient than U.S.-controlled firms in turning over inventories, and more efficient than Other Foreign firms in turning over current assets.

As in the univariate case, the most significant differences emerged in the leverage and liquidity equations, (9) to (12). Regardless of industry, U.S. firms tend to be less levered than other firms, and Canadian-controlled firms are generally less levered than Other Foreign-controlled firms. This result holds for any definition of leverage, and is similar to that derived in Section III-3. U.S.-controlled firms are more liquid when inventories are included in the definition of liquidity (LIQ), but not when inventories are netted out (QCK). It is again apparent that U.S.-controlled firms are relatively inventory intensive and this accounts for their observed liquidity. However, it should be noted that the QCK equation has poor explanatory power.

The dividend equation (not presented) also had poor explanatory power. Not one variable was significant and the $\bar{R}^2$ was less than .01. Therefore, nothing can be said about the comparative dividend behaviour of foreign- and Canadian-controlled firms in the context of this study.

As a final remark, it should be noted that the regression analysis suggests that the differences between Canadian and Other Foreign firms are more limited than was suggested by the univariate analysis. With the exception of some leverage and liquidity variables, Canadian-controlled firms seem to differ from U.S. firms, but not from Other Foreign firms.

III-5 Summary and Conclusions

The results presented in this chapter clearly indicate that there are important financial differences among the U.S., Canadian, and Other Foreign firms represented in the sample. Furthermore, some distinctions can be made between the financial structures of U.S.-controlled and Other Foreign-controlled firms. Indeed, in many respects, the latter more closely resemble Canadian-controlled firms. The concept of a homogeneous, foreign-controlled sector is therefore clearly inappropriate, at least when financial structures are being considered.

The observed financial differences are widespread, although not as widespread as an examination of aggregated data would suggest. The most unambiguous differences are found when leverage and liquidity ratios are considered. U.S.-controlled firms rely least heavily on debt and most heavily on retained earnings. The majority of the debt that they do incur is from affiliated companies. Other Foreign firms, on the other hand, rely most heavily on debt, but do not borrow more from affiliates than do similar Canadian firms. Pattison found that foreign-controlled firms were less debt intensive, and as he did not distinguish between U.S. and Other Foreign firms, his result must be attributed to the dominant weight of U.S.-controlled firms. Pattison also found that foreign-controlled firms tended to borrow more from affiliates, which this study suggests is true only for U.S.-controlled firms. These results suggest that home-country financial norms are relevant to the behaviour of subsidiaries in Canada. Non-American firms are generally more highly levered, and this applies to their subsidiaries in Canada. Capital markets appear to be partially segmented. U.S.-controlled firms apparently avoid incurring debt in the relatively high interest rate Canadian market, relying on affiliate borrowing and retained earnings, while Other Foreign firms seen content to rely more heavily on debt, and do not borrow more from affiliates than do Canadian firms. The last result may be caused by the relative youth of non-American firms and their relative inexperience as MNCs.

U.S.-controlled firms have been found to be the most liquid and Other Foreign-controlled firms the least liquid when all current assets are considered. When inventories are netted out, the U.S. liquidity advantage disappears. Other Foreign firms remain the least liquid, although this difference is not significant according to the regression analysis. In general, U.S.-controlled firms devote a higher percentage of their assets to inventories and receivables, the former being more important than the latter. While this result is apparently consistent with Robbins and Stobaugh's argument that subsidiaries of MNCs will be relatively more inventory intensive, one must be cautious in interpreting the results. For one thing, only U.S. firms have been found to be more inventory intensive than domestic firms; Other Foreign firms do not differ from domestic firms. Furthermore, when inventory turnover is considered, U.S. firms are found not to be significantly less efficient in turning over their inventories than the other control groups, although their inventory turnover ratios are lower. Given the larger average sales volume of U.S. firms, and given that there are likely to be economies of scale to inventory accumulation, it may still be true that U.S. firms tend to over-accumulate inventories. Pattison also found that foreign-controlled firms (considered as a single group) were relatively more inventory intensive, but not necessarily less efficient in turning over inventories. He also found foreign-controlled firms to be more liquid, even when inventories were excluded from current assets, a result which is not confirmed here.

U.S.-controlled firms are more efficient in turning over their total assets, but are not more efficient in turning over current or fixed assets considered separately. As U.S.-controlled firms tend to invest less in other assets, and particularly in affiliated companies, this is the source of their efficiency advantage. Pattison found that foreign-controlled firms tended to invest *more* in affiliates and ascribed this result to the greater flexibility which they have in allocating funds. While this interpretation seems reasonable, the reversal of the basic result in the present study suggests that it may be incorrect. An alternative explanation, given the present findings, might be that subsidiaries of U.S. parents remit funds to the parent for re-allocation, but do not themselves have the authority to invest the funds. Our result might also reflect the fact that U.S. subsidiaries in Canada do not diversify to the extent that their parents or Canadian firms do.

Further evidence supporting this view is provided by the finding that U.S. firms tend to employ a relatively smaller percentage of non-production labour. This could be explained by the truncated nature of subsidiary production. This result, however, does not hold for Other Foreign firms, and is not statistically strong.

In general, support is provided for theories suggesting that subsidiaries of MNCs behave differently from domestic firms, and that these differences are reflected in financial variables, at least where U.S.-controlled firms are concerned. In the case of Other Foreign firms, the evidence is more tenuous. A possible explanation is that non-American firms in general have yet to become truly multinational; they are merely foreign investors, in the sense that they invest abroad, but they have not yet taken on the characteristics of true MNCs. The "American Challenge" may yet be a reality.

Notes

1. Johnson (1978), for example, uses analysis of variance to derive empirically-based categories. The categories employed in Sections III--2 and III-3 may be seen to be consistent with those derived by Johnson.

2. None of the variables discussed in this paragraph correspond to the concept of capital intensity as used in economic theory. The theoretical notion is a physical concept, expressed in units of capital (or labour) input per unit of physical output. The measures calculated from financial data are in dollar terms, and therefore reflect both price and quantity.

3. The same point is made by Naumann-Etienne (1974). The equity problem will arise again in the context of profitability measures.

4. Pattison (1978) used such published data in his study.

5. The tests are two-tailed t-tests which do not assume equal variances between (among) groups. The two-tailed test makes the significance threshold more restrictive, but is employed since there are no a priori expected differences for some variables (e.g., FATA), while for others the a priori considerations are contradictory (e.g., LIQ).

6. This finding tends to support the view that KIT measures capital efficiency, while ULP may be considered as a proxy for capital intensity. There is a slight negative relationship between KIT and ULP. The simple correlation coefficient between these two variables is $-.012$.

7. The quick ratios for Canadian-controlled firms have very high standard deviations, thus suggesting that the improvement in the average QCK may not be considered a general result applying to all such firms.

8. Firm size and firm growth have been identified as determinants of financial structure by Gupta (1969), where a discussion of the rationale for the inclusion of these variables may be found.

9. A regression analysis of this type is similar to performing a separate analysis of variance for each industry. A good discussion of the relationship between regression analysis and analysis of variance is found in Draper and Smith (1966, Ch. 9).

10. For a discussion of the calculation of growth rates, see Chapter VI. The results presented below do not change when the growth of assets is used to measure firm growth.

11. The construction of a separate model for each variable was not possible, given resource and time constraints.

12. In addition, the growth term was rarely significant, and is only reported when it was significant, or nearly so. Although U.S.-controlled firms tend to be relatively faster growing (see Chapter VI), the exclusion of the growth term never changes the sign or significance of the control dummies.

13. When ULT (total labour costs) is used as the dependent variable, the U.S. coefficient is not significant, but is negative. This gives at least weak support to the notion that U.S.-controlled firms use less overhead labour.

14. It should be noted, however, that the growth terms are highly significant in these equations, and as will be shown in Chapter VI, U.S.-controlled firms tend to grow faster than others, when growth is measured by sales.

IV

PATTERNS OF PROFITABILITY

IV-1 Introduction

Profitability is surely one of the most important and widely studied concepts in economics and business. This is true despite some dispute over the measurement and interpretation of profitability. Yet, no one disputes the crucial role played by profits in both allocating resources and serving as a source of investment funds, particularly in market economies. Thus profits are determinants of both the static (allocational) efficiency and the dynamic (growth) potential of an economy.

Economic studies of profitability usually fall into one or more of the following categories:[1]

(1) *Static efficiency:* these studies concentrate on the profitability of given categories of firms, usually firms in different size classes. Profitability and efficiency are often equated in this context, and profitability is therefore interpreted as being a measure of the existence of economies of scale to the firm. Thus, if large firms are found to be more profitable than small firms, this result is taken to be an indicator of the existence of economies of scale.[2] Furthermore, the most profitable size category is taken to represent the optimal sized firm. In this last interpretation, profitability information is usually supplemented by data on the variance of profitability which indicates the certainty of achieving the mean profit rate for that category. The variance of profitability is taken as a proxy for risk, and firms are therefore classified by both pro-

fitability and risk. In general, profitability in this context may be said to reflect "the overall suitability of firms' sizes to their market environment" (Scherer, 1970, p. 79).

(2) *Industrial structure:* the performance (profitability) of a firm may reflect factors other than efficiency. Other determinants of profitability have been identified by industrial economists and are generally referred to as structural variables. Structural variables attempt to represent the market power possessed by the firm (or industry), and include measures of industry concentration, barriers to entry, product differentiation, and tariffs.

(3) *Dynamic:* as profits may serve as a source of funds for reinvestment, and inasmuch as high profitability may facilitate external financing, profitability is often studied within the context of the growth of the firm. Specifically, profitability and growth are often found to be positively related, thus suggesting that high profitability firms will become relatively larger and more powerful than less profitable firms.

The role of industrial structure (and other factors) in explaining inter-firm differences in profitability will constitute the subject matter of Chapter V. The relationship between profitability and the growth of the firm will be analysed in Chapter VI.

The present chapter will compare the patterns of profitability of U.S.-, Other Foreign-, and Canadian-controlled firms in terms suggested by the static efficiency studies. As noted, these studies attempt to judge the viability of different categories of firms, as measured by various aspects of their profitability. Recent literature has focussed on firm size and nationality as relevant categories.[3] The profitability and the stability of profitability of firms of different nationalities has become a subject of interest in Europe, where the process of integration has led to some concern over the most appropriate size of firm to service the expanded market. Concern has also been expressed over the ability of certain firms to continue to exist in the new competitive environment. Related to these issues is the policy problem of whether mergers should be encouraged to promote larger firms, capable of serving European markets more efficiently, and capable of competing with U.S. firms operating in Europe.

Similar concerns have been expressed in Canada. The issues in Canada relate both to the ability of Canadian-controlled firms to compete with foreign-controlled firms in Canada, as well as to the ability of Canadian-based firms to compete abroad. It has already been suggested in Chapter I that the subsidiaries of MNCs will be more profitable than domestic firms and this will be examined in Section IV-3. The comparative analysis of profitability in this section will be undertaken within the size-profitability context, thus allow-ing conclusions regarding the suitability of Canadian-based firms, regardless of country of control, to their economic environment.

Section IV-4 is devoted to an analysis of loss corporations by size and control group. This section begins the analysis of the stability of firms, since it identifies the type of firm which is most (least) likely to incur losses. The analysis of stability is continued in Section IV-5, where profitability over time (1968-1972) is examined. At issue is the relative ability of firms of various categories to maintain their profitability over the business cycle.

Defining profitability for the purposes of empirical application is always a problem, and is more acute when accounting data are employed. Accounting techniques differ from firm to firm and this introduces unknown biases into the measurement of profits.[4] This problem can be mentioned, but not avoided. In addition, however, accounting data offer the possibility of calculating a number of profitability measures, and it is difficult to choose among them, a priori.

This study will employ three measures of profitability: two profit rates and a profit margin. The former are defined on the firms' capital stock or net worth, while the latter is calculated on sales. While profitability measures are connected by accounting identities, and are thus related both theoretically and statistically, different measures are often employed for different purposes. These matters are discussed further in Section IV-2.

IV-2 Measures of Profitability

There are many possible profitability measures which can be calculated from balance sheet data, and there is some disagreement over which of these is the most appropriate measure. Profitability may be measured as a percentage of assets or equity (profit rates), or as a percentage of sales (profit margins). In addition, profits may be calculated net or gross of interest payments and taxes. The measure actually chosen usually depends on the purpose of the analysis as well as the interpretation of the analyst.

As the purpose of this study is to survey broad aspects of profitability, it was decided to rely on more than measure. These are defined in Table IV-1. There are three profitability measures, two profit rates (EBIT and NPK), and one profit margin (GPS). EBIT reflects the return on total capital (assets) and is often interpreted as an index of efficiency. EBIT, which stands for earnings before interest and taxes, includes profits, interest payments and taxes in the numerator. Interest payments are included because the denominator includes debt;

TABLE IV-1

PROFITABILITY MEASURES: DEFINITIONS

Variable	Symbol	Calculation*
Earnings before interest and taxes on total assets	EBIT	42 + 30 + 31 + 32 + 36 / 13
Net profit on capital employed	NPK	42 / 8 + 4 − 16
Gross margin	GPS	22 / 39
Variance of profitability (over time)	V + profitability (eg. VEBIT)	Variance over time
Growth of net profits	AGNP	$\sum\limits_{t=1969}^{1972} (42_t - 42_{t-1}) / 4$

* Numbers refer to those presented in the Appendix to Chapter II.

hence EBIT is a measure which is independent of leverage. Taxes are included because they are in fact part of profits and therefore a guide to the efficiency of the firm. This measure is commonly used by financial analysts and economists who are attempting to measure inter-firm differences in efficiency.

A drawback of EBIT is that it may not reflect the value of a firm in the eyes of its owners, or potential owners. As a consequence, EBIT may not have much value as an index of how financial resources will be allocated. Appropriate measures in this context would be the after-tax rate of return on net worth or equity, or the after-tax rate of return on assets. The latter measure is not much different from EBIT, save that taxes are excluded from the numerator.[5] It has already been argued that equity-based measures of profitability are inappropriate in a context where foreign-owned firms are present, since equity is not an accurate measure of the value of the firm to its owners. Therefore, the measure adopted to reflect these considerations was NPK, defined as the profit rate on capital employed.[6] It is calculated net of interest payments and taxes in the numerator and includes fixed assets and working capital (current assets less current liabilities) in the denominator. This measure, it is felt, will measure the return to long-term capital invested in the firm. The magnitude of the denominator of NPK, it should be noted, lies somewhere between total assets and total equity.

Profit margins are sometimes considered less acceptable as measures of profitability since they measure neither efficiency nor potential returns to owners. Profit margins are dependent on capital efficiency and capacity utilization, and may therefore be misleading.

On the other hand, profit margins may reflect the pricing behaviour of firms, and thus may be useful in examining their ability to exercise market power in augmenting margins. The profit margin selected for this study is GPS, the gross margin. This measure reflects the mark-up on prime costs (labour and materials) and therefore includes overhead expenses as well as interest and taxes. GPS was selected because it has been used in both theoretical and applied research.[7]

As is often the case, these three measures are related. The simple correlation coefficients (r), considered pairwise are:

$$r^{\text{EBIT, NPK}} = .682; \quad r^{\text{EBIT, GPS}} = .439; \quad r^{\text{NPK, GPS}} = .438.$$

The coefficients, all of which are significant at 5%, suggest that firms which are above average according to one measure are also above average according to any other. Indeed, this result applies when other measures of profitability are considered, and is in fact stronger in some cases. In order to ensure that the chosen measures were representative, other profitability indices were calculated. These included rates of return to net worth, rates of return to capital net of taxes, and rates of return to capital which included depreciation as part of profits. It was found that these measures were not only correlated with EBIT, NPK and GPS, but were also correlated with each other. Although correlated variables do not guarantee similar results when a regression analysis is undertaken, it is nevertheless felt that all subsequent results reflect a wide range of profitability measures.

Associated with each profitability measure is its variance over time, denoted as VEBIT, VNPK, or VGPS. The temporal nature of profitability will be discussed in Section IV-5. Before that we will consider the profitability measures averaged over the sample period.

IV-3 Profitability, Foreign Control, and Firm Size

The means of the three profitability measures for each of the three control groups are found in Table IV-2. All variables are averaged over the sample period. An analysis of variance was performed on the means in order to ascertain whether differences in mean values were significant. It is readily apparent that U.S.-controlled firms are more profitable than others, and that in the cases of EBIT and GPS, significantly more profitable. Canadian-controlled firms are more

TABLE IV-2

Profitability Measures, Averaged

Country of Control		EBIT	NPK	GPS
U.S.	m	$12.3^{2, 3}$	12.3^{3}	$24.7^{2, 3}$
	s	9.7	51.0	14.5
OF	m	$7.6^{1, 3}$	12.2	21.6^{1}
	s	4.6	60.2	15.7
CAN	m	$9.0^{1, 2}$	8.2^{1}	21.8^{1}
	s	4.0	17.7	15.3
TOTAL	m	10.4	10.7	23.0
	s	8.1	43.0	15.1

Notes: EBIT, NPK, GPS are averaged over 1968-1972
  U.S. = U.S.-controlled firms
  OF = Other Foreign-controlled firms
  CAN = Canadian-controlled firms

  1 = significantly different from U.S., at 5%, two-tailed test.
  2 = significantly different from OF, at 5%, two-tailed test.
  3 = significantly different from CAN, at 5%, two-tailed test.
  m = mean
  s = standard deviation

profitable than Other Foreign-controlled firms according to EBIT and GPS, although only in the case of EBIT is the difference significant. The NPK measure places Other Foreign firms ahead of Canadian firms, and nearly at the level of U.S. firms. However, this measure exhibits some instability, particularly where Other Foreign firms are concerned. The standard deviation is nearly five times the mean value, and since there are only 90 Other Foreign firms, the mean can be affected by extreme observations. Such extremes were encountered for several Other Foreign firms. In general, NPK is plagued by high standard deviations for all control groups relative to the other measures.

As before, these differences may be caused by other factors and these will be analysed in Chapter V. For the moment, we will isolate the relationship between firm size and profitability. Although all three measures of profitability are employed in this section, it should be noted that EBIT is likely to be the most relevant. If size-profitability studies indicate the suitability of a firm to its economic environment, then EBIT, the efficiency measure of profitability, is preferred as an indicator. GPS and NPK, it will be recalled, do not necessarily measure the efficiency of the firm, but are interpreted as indicators of pricing behaviour or shareholders' welfare.

TABLE IV-3

PROFITABILITY BY SIZE GROUP: ALL FIRMS

Size Group ($000,000)	EBIT		NPK		GPS		
	m	s	m	s	m	s	n
< 5	16.9	13.1	14.7	14.2	21.2	12.5	37
5-10	11.2	9.2	8.6	12.3	23.1	13.3	286
10-20	10.6	11.2	9.0	12.6	23.6	18.3	164
20-40	9.8	11.7	7.8	11.8	22.6	14.0	104
40-80	8.0	9.0	5.5	18.2	22.7	17.7	80
80-160	7.4	6.0	8.3	12.3	23.7	15.2	44
>160	8.8	4.9	8.8	8.6	23.1	11.8	35
Total	10.5	10.1	8.6	13.1	23.0	15.7	750

Notes: m = mean (%)
s = standard deviation (%)
n = number of firms
Size is measured by opening (1968) assets.

In order to provide a frame of reference, we first consider the relationship between firm size and profitability for the entire sample of firms, without making a distinction among control groups. Table IV-3 presents the mean values of the profitability measures by size groups. Here size is measured by opening (1968) size in assets. While there is no relative difference between opening size and average size for this sample, it is customary to employ opening size in profit studies. This avoids any possible interaction between profitability (or any other financial variable) and size over the period. Unless otherwise indicated, size will henceforth be measured in this manner.

It can be seen that the profitability measures behave somewhat differently. EBIT declines steadily with size, although it turns up at the largest size class. NPK behaves in a similar manner, save that it turns up earlier. In neither case, however, do the very largest firms achieve the profit rates of the smaller firms (which comprise a numerical majority of the sample). No discernible trend is visible for GPS. Another interesting feature of Table IV-3 is that the within-class standard deviations do not decline uniformly with size. In other words, there is no systematic tendency for relatively larger firms to have narrower dispersions of profit measures, although the exact relationship differs according to the measure. It is true, however, that the very largest size class exhibits the lowest standard deviation in every case.

While the size-profitability relationship is not particularly surprising, given recent evidence from other countries, the behaviour of the standard deviations is unexpected. It is generally found that intra-group standard deviations decline with firm size.[8] This implies that larger firms are more likely to achieve their group average rate of profit, and are therefore considered less risky. The decline of standard deviations with increasing size is often explained by the "square-root rule", whereby under certain assumptions one expects the standard deviation of profitability to decline inversely with the square root of the proportionate size differential. For example, quadrupling the size of the firm would be expected to halve the variability of profitability. This "rule" is based on the assumption that firms of different sizes are independent, and that large firms may be considered equivalent to a collection of smaller firms. While profit variability has been found to decline with size, "the rate of decline in variability is in reality very much different from the square-root rule" and "by no means as rapid as would occur if large firms consisted simply of independent smaller units" (Prais, 1976, p. 94). Prais shows that the empirical results can be explained by relaxing the independence assumption. However, the results presented in Table IV-3 cannot be explained by the square-root rule, even in its amended version, since there is no over-all tendency for the standard deviations to fall.

The pattern of profitability is not uniform amongst the control groups, as can be seen from Table IV-4. The foreign-controlled firms conform to the over-all pattern found in Table IV-3, in that for EBIT and NPK profitability declines with size up to the largest size categories. For Canadian firms, the pattern is somewhat irregular, but there is no tendency for profitability to increase at very large size groups. Perhaps more important, Table IV-4 reveals that U.S.-controlled firms are more profitable than Canadian-controlled firms according to each measure of profitability in every size category except the $80-160 million range. U.S.-controlled firms are also more profitable than Other Foreign-controlled firms in nearly every category, while Canadian and Other Foreign firms seem to exhibit no pattern. Furthermore, it can be seen that the standard deviation of U.S.-profitability is lower than that for Canadian firms, and this persists in most size categories, for any profitability measure. Other Foreign firms follow mixed patterns which are difficult to summarize, as they depend on the measure of profitability. U.S.- and Canadian-controlled firms are clearly different with respect to the level, variability, and pattern of profitability by size group. U.S. firms are more profitable and are characterized by less variable profits, when compared with Canadian firms of similar size. Other Foreign firms can-

TABLE IV-4

SIZE AND PROFITABILITY BY CONTROL GROUPS

Size Category (000,000)	EBIT						NPK						GPS						n		
	U.S.A.		OF		CAN		U.S.A.		OF		CAN		U.S.A.		OF		CAN		U.S.A.	OF	CAN
	m	s	m	s	m	s	m	s	m	s	m	s	m	s	m	s	m	s			
1. <5	19.8	15.6	X	X	12.2	8.2	18.0	16.0	X	X	9.2	10.6	23.6	13.6	X	X	18.2	11.3	20	2	15
2. 5-10	13.0	9.2	9.7	7.7	9.5	9.1	10.1	10.4	5.2	13.1	7.7	13.8	25.4	15.1	21.2	8.2	21.0	11.6	137	26	123
3. 10-20	12.9	10.5	8.3	5.0	8.5	13.3	9.5	9.0	8.6	15.9	8.6	14.9	25.3	15.5	24.3	12.7	21.0	22.9	78	25	61
4. 20-40	11.2	7.5	4.7	6.8	9.9	17.0	8.8	7.0	4.0	8.7	7.9	17.3	23.8	13.4	15.5	14.9	23.9	13.8	53	15	36
5. 40-80	9.9	9.7	5.2	4.9	7.3	9.9	7.7	12.4	4.6	10.9	2.8	28.2	24.4	13.4	22.6	26.4	20.1	15.5	37	19	24
6. 80-160	7.6	4.3	4.4	4.1	8.3	7.8	7.6	11.0	6.3	13.3	9.8	13.7	23.5	16.3	18.1	10.8	26.2	15.5	19	7	18
7. >160	10.5	5.5	9.6	4.1	6.1	2.9	8.8	5.7	18.5	21.0	5.8	3.3	23.5	12.4	31.1	16.3	20.2	8.8	18	4	13
8. Total	12.4	9.7	7.6	6.6	9.0	11.1	9.8	10.3	6.7	13.4	7.6	15.7	24.7	14.6	21.6	15.7	21.4	15.3	362	98	290

Notes: X = omitted to preserve confidentiality
See Table IV-3 for definitions of symbols.

not be so simply characterized in the context of the present analysis.

More information is provided through the use of regression analysis, with a profitability measure being the dependent variable, and size (or size squared) the independent variable. It was found that the logarithm of size usually provided a better fit, and thus the estimated equations take the form,

$$P = a + b_1 \text{Log Size, or}$$
$$P = a + b_1 \text{Log Size} + b_2 \text{Log Size}^2$$

where size is opening size, measured in assets and P is a profitability measure.

Selected regression equations are found in Table IV-5, for all sample firms. In a cross-section analysis, the existence of heteroscedasticity is always a possibility, particularly when firm size measures are involved.[9] For each of the equations estimated in Table IV-5, a heteroscedasticity check was run. The absolute value of the residual of each equation was computed and the Spearman Rank Correlation Coefficient was computed between this value and the measure of size.[10] In none of the cases was there any evidence of heteroscedasticity, and thus no weighting was deemed necessary. This result is not surprising, given the behaviour of the intra-group standard deviations encountered in Table IV-3.

The regression results basically confirm the relationships indicated in Table IV-3. No discernable relationship between GPS and size is found, the coefficients on the size terms being insignificant.

TABLE IV-5

SIZE AND PROFITABILITY: SELECTED REGRESSION EQUATIONS

(ALL FIRMS)

Independent Variable	EBIT	EBIT	GPS	GPS	NPK	NPK
OSL	−.01322*	−.09706*	.01459	.02822	−.00589	−.08381
	(.00322)	(.04397)	(.04266)	(.06651)	(.00421)	(.05749)
OSL²		.00405*		−.00132		.00377
		(.00212)		(.00321)		(.00277)
constant	.23339	.66016	.03004	.08209	.14285	.53948
R̄²	.0220	.0268	.0001	.0003	.0026	.0057
F	16.82	10.27	.05	.11	1.95	1.90
(d.o.f.)	(1,749)	(2,748)	(1,749)	(2,748)	(1,749)	(2,748)

Notes: numbers in parentheses are standard errors
 * = significant at 5% (two-tailed test)
 OSL = opening size (assets), logs

The size-profitability relationship for both EBIT and NPK is best described by a parabolic curve. In both cases the over-all relationship is negative, but profitability does turn up at very large size.[11] In the case of EBIT, the relationship is significant, while in the case of NPK the coefficients approach significance at the 10% level. In all cases, however, the degree of explanatory power of the equations is low, even when the estimated coefficients are significantly different from zero. This indicates that there are other factors which contribute to the explanation of inter-firm differences in profitability.

Size-profitability equations were also estimated by control group and these results are found in Table IV-6. As was the case for the entire sample, the explanatory power of these equations is very weak. Even so, some differences amongst the control groups do exist, particularly in the case of EBIT. Whereas both foreign-controlled groups conform to the over-all parabolic relationship for EBIT-size, the relationship is negative (although insignificant) for Canadian-controlled firms. EBIT, therefore, tends to turn up for large foreign-controlled firms, but not for those which are Canadian-controlled. The same is true for NPK, although the coefficients are not significant for Other Foreign and Canadian firms. No significant coefficients are found in the GPS equations.

By dividing the sample into sub-groups, it was possible to perform the Chow test on the equality of regression coefficients (see Johnston, 1972, p. 207). The resulting F-statistics on slope and intercept terms provide the summary conclusions illustrated in Table IV-7. It can be seen that the slope coefficients are significantly different from the over-all relationship only in the case of EBIT, and then only at the 10% level. The intercept differences are significant at 5% for all measures except NPK. The results suggest that Canadian- and foreign-controlled firms are not significantly different when the shape of the size-profitability relationship is considered (except in the case of EBIT), but that the intercept terms (the profitability differential for any size class) are different.[12]

We conclude, therefore, that U.S.-controlled firms are generally more profitable than either Canadian- or foreign-controlled firms, and this result holds for most size classes. In addition, U.S.-controlled firms exhibit a lower standard deviation of profit rates, and this is true for most size classes. Over-all, the relationship between size and profitability in Canada depends on the measure of profitability. For EBIT, the measure most related to efficiency, the relationship is parabolic, i.e., EBIT declines with size up to the largest size classes. The intra-group standard deviation of EBIT is lowest for the very largest firms. However, this over-all relationship masks the fact that EBIT declines continuously with size for Canadian-con-

TABLE IV-6

SIZE AND PROFITABILITY: SELECTED REGRESSION EQUATIONS
(BY CONTROL GROUP)

Independent Variable	Dependent Variable EBIT			NPK			GPS		
	U.S.	OF	CAN	U.S.	OF	CAN	U.S.	OF	CAN
OSL	−.14132*	−.23815*	−.00812	0.15072*	−.14898	−.00265	−.00425	−.17259	.12688
	(.05728)	(.08471)	(.00578)	(.06146)	(.18344)	(.00820)	(.00670)	(.21578)	(.11444)
OSL²	.00602*	.01073*		.00673*	.00741			.00840	−.00581
	(.00274)	(.00409)		(.00294)	(.00877)			(.01043)	(.00556)
constant	.92115	1.37098	.16914	.91852	.80725	−.06616	.28876	1.09125	−.46174
R̄²	.0484	.1385	.0068	.0281	.0084	.0004	.0011	.0068	.0069
F	9.13	7.63	1.97	5.18	.40	.10	.40	.33	.99
( )	(2,359)	(2.95)	(1,288)	(2,359)	(2.95)	(1,288)	(1,360)	(2.95)	(2,287)

Notes: See Table IV-5

TABLE IV-7

CHOW TEST RESULTS

	EBIT	NPK	GPS
intercept	Yes*	Yes**	Yes*
slope	Yes**	No	No

Notes: Tests were based on the following equations:
1) $EBIT = a + b_1\,OSL + b_2\,OSL^2$
2) $NPK = a + b_1\,OSL + b_2\,OSL^2$
3) $GPS = a + b_1\,OSL + b_2\,OSL^2$

Yes indicates that the control group equations differ in slope or intercept from the total sample equation.
No indicates that the control group equations did not differ in slope or intercept from the total sample equation.
*   = significant at 5%
** = significant at 10%
See Johnston (1972, p. 207) for a discussion of the Chow test.

trolled firms. EBIT turns up only for the largest foreign-controlled firms. The same result is broadly true of NPK, although it may be considered very weak. GPS, while being higher for U.S.-controlled firms, does not vary with size.

In the Canadian environment, it would seem that large size is not an advantage, unless the firm is foreign-controlled. Large firms are in general not above average in profitability, although the very largest firms are more certain of achieving the group mean. Large, foreign-controlled firms are, however, both above average in profitability and more certain of realizing their profits. A policy designed to encourage large Canadian-controlled firms would seem to provide them with no relative advantage should the patterns found here tend to persist.

As a final comment, we note that the analysis has thus far ignored the industry composition of the sample. Industry will be explicitly accounted for in Chapter V. Nevertheless, the basic result that U.S.-controlled firms are more profitable is not changed when industry is examined. U.S.-controlled firms are more profitable in most two-digit industries, for any measure of profitability. U.S. firms are more profitable in 53-68% of the two-digit industries represented in the sample, depending on the profitability measure.[13]

IV-4 Loss Corporations

The discussion of profitability in Section IV-3 ignored the distinction between companies which earned positive profits and those

TABLE IV-8

Number of Loss Corporation by Size Class, Annual

Size Class (000,000)	1968				1969				1970				1971				1972				AVERAGE			
	U.S.	OF	CAN	TOT	U.S.	OF	CAN	TOT	U.S.	OF	CAN	TOT	U.S.	OF	CAN	TOT	U.S.	OF	CAN	TOT	U.S	OF	CAN	TOT
1. <5	0	0	0	0	0	0	1	1	4	0	1	5	1	0	1	2	0	0	3	3	1	0	1	2
2. 5-10	6	0	3	9	9	0	5	14	7	3	17	27	6	3	16	25	11	5	16	32	11	9	16	36
3. 10-20	3	1	0	4	0	2	4	6	7	1	7	15	7	1	6	14	9	3	10	22	8	2	12	22
4. 20-40	2	0	0	2	2	1	3	6	2	1	3	6	8	4	3	15	1	2	7	10	4	6	4	14
5. 40-80	1	0	0	1	0	0	1	1	3	3	2	8	1	2	3	6	5	3	5	13	4	7	4	15
6. 80-160	1	0	0	1	1	0	0	1	3	1	0	4	1	1	3	5	1	1	2	4	3	3	2	8
7. >160	0	0	1	1	0	0	0	0	1	0	0	1	0	0	3	3	1	0	1	2	1	0	1	2
8. TOTAL	13	1	4	18	12	3	14	29	27	9	30	66	24	11	35	70	28	14	44	86	32	27	40	99

Notes: U.S. = U.S.-controlled firms
 OF   = Other Foreign-Controlled firms
 CAN = Canadian-controlled firms
 TOT = total, all firms

that made losses. This section is designed to provide the reader with some information on the extent to which loss corporations exist in the sample, and their distribution by size and control categories.

Table IV-8 summarizes the relevant information. It indicates the number of companies, by control group, which experienced losses in any year over 1968-1972, and the number of firms whose average profits over the five-year period were negative.

Several important points emerge for this table:

(1) The number of loss firms increased consistently over the period, moving counter-cyclically after 1970. However, the fastest rate of increase in the number of loss corporations occurred in 1969-70 as the economy troughed.

(2) While loss firms were numerically concentrated in the lower size classes, as expected, there is no particular pattern when proportions are considered. The percentage of loss firms in any size category and in any year differs from category to category and from year to year. There is no tendency for the percentage of loss corporations to decline with size. On average, the largest proportion of losses is in the 40 to 160 million range, while the lowest percentages are found at the extremes. This is illustrated below:

*Size Category (000,000)	Loss Corporations (%) / Total Loss Corporations	Loss Corporations (%) / Corporations in that Size Category
<5	2	5
5-10	36	13
10-20	22	13
20-40	14	13
40-80	15	19
80-160	8	18
>160	2	6

* These figures are derived from Table IV-8, using averaged data.

Thus, the greatest chance of loss occurs amongst some of Canada's largest corporations.

(3) The number of Canadian-controlled firms suffering losses in all years and all categories, except 1968, is disproportionately high, and rose throughout the period. U.S. firms were below average in experiencing losses in any year, while Other Foreign firms suffered losses in approximate proportion to their representation in the total sample.

(4) The picture changes when the averages are considered. While U.S. firms remain under-represented, Other Foreign firms are greatly over-represented, and Canadian firms are slightly over-represented. It would appear that Other-Foreign firms which sustain losses in any year are the same firms, i.e., their losses tend to persist. Canadian firms, while most likely to incur losses in any given year, may not see these losses persist. This reinforces the view that Other Foreign firms are not yet completely secure in the Canadian market, probably owing to their relative youth. New firms might be expected to sustain losses for several years as capital is put in place and the new market is tapped.

It may be concluded that U.S. firms are not only more profitable, but that they are less likely to experience and sustain losses. However, the higher profitability of U.S. firms cannot be explained by the higher incidence of loss firms amongst the other control groups. When the loss firms are excluded from the sample, the U.S. firms remain more profitable. Furthermore, the over-all size-profitability relationship is not altered. Table IV-9 exhibits the profitability of each size class and control group when the loss firms are eliminated from the sample.[14] Comparing this table with Tables IV-2 and IV-3 reveals that U.S. firms remain more profitable, except in the case of NPK, and that the size-profitability relationship is not altered. As before, GPS exhibits no particular trend, while EBIT and NPK tend to decline up to the largest size classes.

It is beyond the scope of this study to examine why loss corporations are found in disproportionate numbers in any category. More important, the results of this section do indicate that U.S. firms experience relative profit stability.

As there is no good reason to exclude loss corporations from the sample, they are included for the remainder of this study.

IV-5 Profitability Over Time

We now turn to an examination of profitability patterns over the sample period. In particular, we are interested in the temporal variations in profitability of the control groups. The variation in profitability over time indicates the stability of a firm, and is often used as a proxy for risk.[15] Risk, in turn, is thought to be related to the *level* of profitability, a topic considered in Chapter V.

The profitability measures, by control group and year, are presented in Table IV-10. Over-all, it is of interest to note that 1968 did not represent the peak profitability year for this sample, although this was the case for the economy as a whole. Profitability peaked in

TABLE IV-9

PROFITABILITY AND SIZE: EXCLUDING LOSS CORPORATIONS

Size Class (000,000)	EBIT				NPK				GPS			
	U.S.	OF	CAN	TOT	U.S.	OF	CAN	TOT	U.S.	OF	CAN	TOT
1. <5	20.8	X	13.0	17.8	19.0	X	10.8	15.9	24.5	X	18.8	22.0
2. 5-10	14.5	14.0	11.5	13.2	11.7	11.9	10.8	11.3	26.8	23.7	22.5	24.7
3. 10-20	14.4	9.1	11.8	12.6	11.2	11.2	11.8	11.4	26.9	24.1	25.3	25.9
4. 20-40	12.0	8.6	13.3	12.1	10.0	9.2	11.6	10.5	24.9	22.2	25.1	24.2
5. 40-80	12.1	8.0	8.9	10.4	10.3	10.2	3.9	8.3	26.1	21.6	22.1	24.1
6. 80-160	8.6	6.3	9.6	8.8	6.2	12.5	11.9	9.5	25.7	19.4	27.9	26.0
7. >160	11.2	9.6	6.4	9.3	9.5	18.5	6.3	9.5	23.8	31.1	20.1	23.3
8. TOTAL	13.8	10.3	11.3	12.5	11.2	11.7	10.4	11.0	26.0	23.4	23.4	24.7

Notes: X = excluded to preserve confidentiality

TABLE IV-10

PROFITABILITY OVER TIME

		1968	1969	1970	1971	1972	Variance, 1968-1972
EBIT	U.S.	11.7[2,3]	13.1[2,3]	11.4[2,3]	12.4[2,3]	13.2[2,3]	.52
	OF	7.0[1,3]	7.5[1,3]	6.0[1,3]	8.2[1]	9.2[1]	1.17
	CAN	10.1[1,2]	10.5[1,2]	8.0[1,2]	7.7[1]	9.2[1]	1.22
	TOTAL	10.5	11.3	9.4	10.1	11.2	.58
NPK	U.S.	11.6[3]	12.7[2,3]	11.4[2,3]	12.7[3]	13.5[3]	.61
	OF	11.1[3]	11.8[1,3]	10.1[1,3]	13.1[3]	14.3[3]	2.18
	CAN	8.9[1,2]	9.1[1,2]	7.3[1,2]	7.6[1,2]	9.3[1,2]	.68
	TOTAL	10.4	11.1	9.5	10.6	11.4	.43
GPS	U.S.	24.5[3]	25.4[2,3]	24.5[2,3]	24.6[3]	24.8[2,3]	.11
	OF	22.4	22.6[1]	21.5[1]	23.4	17.9[1]	3.71
	CAN	22.2[1]	23.3[1]	21.6[1]	20.7[1]	19.3[1]	1.84
	TOTAL	23.3	24.2	23.0	22.9	21.8	.59

Notes: See Table IV-2
The variance is calculated on the group averages (for five years).

1969, declined in 1970 and rose thereafter, at least for NPK and EBIT. The post-1969 pattern conforms to the behaviour of the economy as a whole, as noted in Chapter II.[16]

U.S.-controlled firms maintained their profitability advantage in all years and for all measures, except for NPK in 1971 and 1972. In addition, U.S.-controlled firms on average exhibited more stability over the period, for all measures, than either Canadian or Other Foreign firms. The relative stability of profitability for the latter depends on the measure employed. In particular, U.S. margins remained remarkably stable over the period as compared to the other groups. Both Canadian and Other Foreign firms saw their margins decline in 1972 which contributed to their relatively high variances.

When the variance of profitability is calculated using individual firms as observations, the same conclusion emerges: U.S. firms are more stable. These calculations are found in Table IV-11. The variance of profitability is significantly lower for U.S.-controlled firms, regardless of the measure. Canadian- and Other Foreign-controlled firms have less stable profits than do U.S. firms, and they are not different from each other according to VNPK and VGPS. This result parallels that arrived at in the analysis of profitability where it was found that U.S.-controlled were in general more profitable than either Canadian or Other Foreign firms. The latter were found not to differ from each other according to NPK and GPS measures. However, when EBIT is examined, Other Foreign firms are found to be less profitable, but less risky, than Canadian firms.

TABLE IV-11

VARIANCE AND GROWTH OF PROFITABILITY

Country of Control		VEBIT (%)	VNPK (%)	VGPS (%)	AGNP (%)
U.S.	m	.6[2, 3]	.1[2, 3]	12.7[2, 3]	5.5
	s	1.5	.3	14.6	15.0
OF	m	1.3[1, 3]	3.6[1]	60.3[1]	5.6
	s	1.6	35.4	182.4	19.2
CAN	m	1.9[1, 2]	1.1[1]	26.9[1]	3.6
	s	17.6	19.2	33.9	18.2
TOTAL	m	1.0	.9	26.1	4.8
	s	11.0	17.5	53.2	17.2

Notes: See Table IV-2.

Table IV-11 also presents the average annual rate of growth of net profits for each control group over the sample period (AGNP). While the foreign-controlled firms witnessed more rapidly growing profits than Canadian firms, the differences were not significant.

The variance of profitability by size group is calculated in Table IV-12. There is a broad, although irregular, tendency for the variance to decline with size.[17] It is certainly true that the largest firms, those with assets exceeding $160 million, have the lowest variances for all measures, and may be considered the most stable by this measure. This accords with our previous findings regarding the stability of the very largest firms. A similar pattern emerges by control group, save that the variance of U.S.-controlled firms in most size categories is lower than that of the other firms.

A question related to the stability of profitability is whether patterns of profitability tend to persist over time. Put another way, did firms which began the sample period with above average profitability, tend to maintain their relative advantage at the end of the period? In particular, we wish to ascertain whether U.S.-controlled firms maintained their profitability advantage.

This question has not been addressed with any frequency in the economics literature. One of the few attempts was undertaken by Whittington (1971), who found that profitability did tend to persist over two time periods in the United Kingdom. His procedure took the following regression form:

$$\pi_t = a + b\pi_{t-1}$$

where π represents a profitability measure, and t is time. His data on

TABLE IV-12

VARIANCE OF PROFITABILITY BY SIZE GROUP

Size Category (00,000)	VEBIT m(%)	VNPK m(%)	VGPS m(%)
<5	.9	1.0	1.9
5-10	.9	1.2	20.5
10-20	.7	1.0	49.1
20-40	3.4	.5	8.2
40-80	.5	.7	22.2
80-160	.2	.4	1.7
>160	.2	.3	1.2
Total	1.0	.9	26.1

Notes: See Table IV-3.

profitability were averaged over one time period (t) and regressed on average profitability in a prior time period (t− 1). Thus, two distinct time periods were employed by Whittington. If the estimated b is between 0 and 1, then there is a tendency for above average profit firms in t− 1 to remain above average in t, but by a lesser amount. There is a regression towards the mean which, if the persistance continued over a long enough period, would result in all firms having the same profitability. Whittington found in fact that b was positive, and less than one, with the above implications.

These points are illustrated in Figure IV-1 where profitability in the current period (t) is plotted against profitability in a prior period (t−1). The legend indicates how any firm would stand in relation to the mean profitability ($\bar{\pi}$) in either period. If all firms which were above the mean in t−1 were also above average in t, then all the observations would lie in quadrants I or III and an estimated regression line would be as indicated in Figure IV-2. On the other hand, if all firms which were above average in t−1 fell below the average in t, and all those below the average in t−1 rose to be above average in t, then all observations would lie in quadrants II and IV.

In reality, of course, these extreme cases are not observed. Rather, elements of both cases exist. However, if the over-all relationship is positive, then we approximate Case (i) and if the over-all relation is negative, then we approximate Case (ii). In fact, Whittington found

Figure IV-1

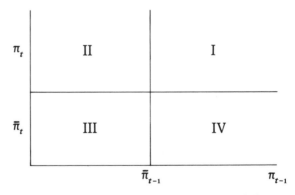

Quadrants I, II :   above average profitability in t
III, IV : below average profitability in t
I, IV :   above average profitability in t-1
II, III : below average profitability in t-1

Figure IV-2

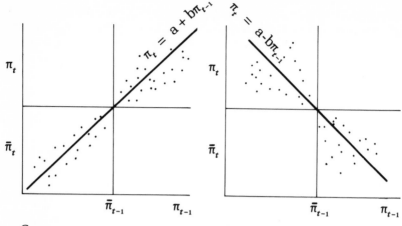

Case
(i) Above average firms
   remain above average and
   below average firms
   remain below average.

Case
(ii) Below average firms
   become above average and
   above average firms
   become below average.

the relationship to be positive and hence concluded that above average firms tend to remain so and vice-versa.

If we rotate the regression line of Case (i) in a clockwise manner, it is clear that whatever the spread of the observations in $t-1$, they will have narrowed in t. That is, a firm which was well above $\bar{\pi}_{t-1}$ would still be above $\bar{\pi}_t$, but by a lesser amount (and vice versa). This is the meaning of the statement—that there is regression towards the mean, and it occurs if $0 < b < 1$.

Unfortunately, we have only one time period with which to work, and it is therefore impossible to repeat Whittington's test. A "second best" test has been attempted, although it must be approached with caution. Our data permit only the estimation of the following equation:

$$\pi_{72} = a + b\,\pi_{68}$$

where, as before, π is a profitability measure.

In other words, we are replacing two distinct time periods with the opening and closing year profitability. This is obviously not a completely satisfactory procedure, since one year may produce random variations in profitability.[18] Nevertheless, the test is not meaningless since 1968 and 1972 are comparable; both are pre-peak profitability years. For this sample, profitability peaked in 1969, while for all firms profitability continued to rise after 1972.

Table IV-13 presents the regression results. For all firms it can be seen that there is a definite tendency for profitability to persist for all measures except NPK. The NPK coefficient, however, is not significant. For EBIT and GPS it is true that firms which began the period with above average profitability also ended the period with above average profitability, but their advantage had been eroded (b is less than 1 in all cases).[19]

TABLE IV-13

THE PERSISTENCE OF PROFITABILITY: REGRESSION EQUATIONS

All Firms	EBIT72	=	.058 +	.513* EBIT68	$\bar{R}^2 = .152$
				(.044)	
	GPS72	=	.034 +	.788* GPS68	$\bar{R}^2 = .182$
				(.061)	
	NPK72	=	.010 −	.002 NPK68	$\bar{R}^2 = .000$
				(.013)	
U.S. Firms	EBIT72	=	.069 +	.539* EBIT68	$\bar{R}^2 = .240$
				(.050)	
	GPS72	=	.067 +	.740* GPS68	$\bar{R}^2 = .667$
				(.028)	
	NPK72	=	.061 +	.455* NPK68	$\bar{R}^2 = .078$
				(.081)	
OF Firms	EBIT72	=	.062 +	.422* EBIT68	$\bar{R}^2 = .130$
				(.112)	
	GPS72	=	.040 +	.620* GPS68	$\bar{R}^2 = .049$
				(.279)	
	NPK72	=	.081 +	.188 NPK68	$\bar{R}^2 = .004$
				(.284)	
CAN Firms	EBIT72	=	.045 +	.471* EBIT68	$\bar{R}^2 = .094$
				(.086)	
	GPS72	=	−.007 +	.899* GPS68	$\bar{R}^2 = .142$
				(.130)	
	NPK72	=	.099 −	.006 NPK68	$\bar{R}^2 = .000$
				(.018)	

Notes: figures in parentheses are standard errors.
  * = significant at 5% (two-tailed test)
  ** = significant at 10% (two-tailed test)

If the pattern suggested by the all-firm equations were representative, it would certainly suggest that the profitability gap among firms would tend to close. In particular, Canadian-controlled firms would, over time, become as profitable as U.S.-controlled firms. Consider the all-firm EBIT equation. In 1968, an average U.S. firm had EBIT = 11.7%, while an average Canadian firm had EBIT = 10.1%, a difference of 1.6%. According to the EBIT equation, the U.S. firm's EBIT in 1972 would be 11.8%, while the Canadian firm's EBIT would be 11.0%, a difference of .8%. Therefore the profitability gap would have narrowed.

In fact, this did not occur because the persistence patterns of the control groups were different. This is seen by examining the equations estimated by control group. The Chow test indicates that the control groups differ by intercept and not by slope, at least for EBIT and GPS.[20] This result suggests that while there is a tendency for intra-group regression towards the mean, the inter-group differences will persist. Thus, over the period, there was no tendency for inter-group profitability differences to disappear. Whether these patterns persisted into the post-1972 period remains an interesting question.

One would expect there to be differences in the persistence of profitability by size class, with larger firms exhibiting greater stability. The persistence equations were accordingly estimated by size category. The estimated coefficients showed no over-all tendency to increase with size, and were often insignificant. However, the largest size category (over $160 million in assets) exhibited significant coefficients which were close to 1, indicating that the largest firms tended to maintain their profitability levels. Again, this is reflective of the greater temporal stability of profitability of the very largest firms.

IV-6 Summary and Conclusions

The evidence produced in this chapter points to the unmistakable conclusion that the profitability performance of U.S.-controlled firms in Canada has been superior to that of other firms. U.S.-controlled firms are more profitable, experience greater profit stability, and are less likely to incur losses. This conclusion holds true for all measures of profitability considered, and for the variation in these measures, calculated within groups, or over time.

These characteristics of U.S.-controlled firms may be attributable to their being subsidiaries of U.S. multinational corporations. But they are not characteristics of all subsidiaries. Foreign subsidiaries in Canada which are controlled by non-U.S. parents are certainly less profitable than subsidiaries of U.S.-parents, and are most probably less profitable than Canadian-controlled firms. In addition, Other Foreign-controlled firms are more likely to incur losses and exhibit a high, if not the highest, degree of profit instability. In general, Other Foreign-controlled firms' pattern of profitability most resembles that of Canadian-controlled firms, and both are different from U.S.-controlled firms. It would appear that national characteristics, as opposed to multinational characteristics, are most important in determining patterns of profitability. As was the case with financial structures, it cannot be concluded that all foreign-controlled firms in Canada may be considered as a homogeneous group.

Over-all, size confers few, if any, advantages to all but the very largest firms. Over most size classes, increasing firm size brings with it neither an increase in profit rates, nor a decrease in variability. The very largest firms in the sample achieve the most stable profit rates and profit margins, and are less likely to incur losses. To this extent, very large size is advantageous for all firms, regardless of country of control. The largest foreign-controlled firms, while not the most profitable, are more profitable than the next largest, foreign-controlled group. This is not the case for Canadian-controlled firms, for which profitability declines continuously with size.

Put in other terms, policies designed to promote large firms in manufacturing will not create more viable firms unless the firms so created are very large by Canadian standards. In addition, the creation of very large Canadian-controlled firms, should these patterns persist, would still not guarantee their ability to compete with U.S.-controlled firms in Canada.

Finally, we note that over the sample period, there was a tendency for profit rates to regress towards the mean, and this applies to both Canadian- and foreign-controlled firms. More important, they are regressing toward different means which implies that Canadian-U.S. profitability differentials persisted over the period, and may persist into the future.

Notes

1. This typology is due to Eatwell (1971).

2. When firms are used as the unit of observation, then the economies of scale include production, distribution, marketing, and financing advantages, whereas when plants are studied, only production economies are relevant. In the case of firms, there is some dispute over the interpretation of distribution, marketing, and financial advantages,

should they exist. The problem is whether such economies are real or pecuniary. See, for example, the Demsetz-Weiss exchange in Goldschmid (1974).

3. The firm size-profitability studies, and their relevance, are surveyed by Eatwell (1971). For an example of a study using firms' size and nationality, see Jacquemin and Cardon (1973). While Eatwell suggests that large firms tend to be more profitable, the post-1971 literature casts considerable doubt on this conclusion. For the U.S., see Shepherd (1972) and Baldwin (1974); for France, Jenny and Weber (1974); for the U.K., Whittington (1971); for Europe as a whole, Jacquemin and Cardon. A discussion of the relevance of these results in a European Context is found in Jacquemin and de Jong (1977).

4. See Weiss (1974, p. 196-199) for a brief discussion of these problems.

5. In fact EBIT and its post-tax counterpart were found to be nearly perfectly collinear. Indeed, even the subtraction of interest payments left EBIT and the post-tax, post-interest rate of return on assets nearly perfectly collinear.

6. This measure is often employed by Statistics Canada in various publications.

7. Most recently, both Eichner (1973) and Wood (1975) have made gross margins central elements in theories of firm behaviour. McFetridge (1973), in his study of inter-industry differences in profitability in Canada, used a markup variable similar to GPS.

8. See Prais (1976, p. 96-97). He shows, however, that the rate of decline is modest at the size levels considered in this study.

9. Heteroscedasticity occurs when the variance of the disturbance term is not constant. This can occur because variable values and their variations are related.

10. See Johnston (1972), p. 219 for a discussion of this method.

11. For EBIT, profitability turns up at an asset size of about 162 million dollars. Only 35 of 750 firms fall in this range. For NPK the turning point is about 70 million dollars, and 120 firms are in this range. Thus, a minority of firms may be said to possess an advantage from size.

12. This point will be taken up again in Chapter V.

13. However, no significant size-profitability relationship of any form could be found in industry equations. This result is similar to one reported by Marcus (1969) for the United States, where a positive over-all size-profitability relationship disappeared when the firms were considered by industry. In the present case, the Chow-test indicated that industry affected the intercept, but not the slope of the equations.

14. The loss firms so excluded are the firms which experience negative *average* profits over the five-year period.

15. Recent literature has proposed other measures of risk, based on capital asset pricing models. These measures, called beta coefficients, are founded on the relationship of a particular asset to a market portfolio of

assets. A textbook exposition of these ideas is found in Clark, Clark and Elgers (1976). Data limitations prevented the use of beta coefficients.

16. It should also be pointed out that for the economy as a whole profitability continued to rise in the post-1972 period, peaking in 1973-1974.

17. A regression of the variance of profitability on firm size (or its logarithm) produced coefficients which were negative, but barely significant at 10%.

18. The use of two different time periods is not without its problems since the choice of such periods is often quite arbitrary.

19. Of course, the reverse is also true. Firms which began the period with below average profitability, also ended the period in such condition, but their relative disadvantage was reduced.

20. The NPK equations are obviously different among the control groups, but their low degree of explanatory power in all cases leaves them suspect.

V

THE DETERMINANTS OF PROFITABILITY

V-1 Introduction

Industrial economists have developed a methodology for analysing inter-firm or inter-industry differences in profitability. This methodology, the genesis of which is attributed to Joe Bain, was designed to examine the impact of market structure on industry profitability.[1] Specifically, it is suggested that profitability is enhanced in those industries where collusion is possible, where barriers to entry exist, or where competition is otherwise impeded. The same basic methodology has been applied to the study of firm profitability. In the case of firms, firm and industry characteristics are both admitted into the analysis.[2] Inter-firm differences in profitability are therefore attributed partly to the characteristics of the firm itself and partly to the competitive circumstances of the industry to which it belongs.

Unfortunately, the interpretation of the role of some variables, notably firm size, in those models has generated some controversy. For example, Hall and Weiss (1967) found a positive relationship between firm size and profitability, and interpreted it as an indication of barriers to entry (a structural phenomenon) rather than the efficiency advantages of large firms. Some economists have challenged this interpretation, suggesting that large firms are more efficient than small firms (Demsetz, 1974).

The type of model discussed above will be introduced in this chapter. The model is defined and discussed in Section V-2. The model will be used to analyse and compare the profitability positions of Canadian- and foreign-controlled firms. Specifically, we wish to ascertain whether the observed profitability advantage· of U.S.-controlled firms persists when explicit account is taken of market structure, firm size, risk and industry composition. It should be noted that such an analysis has not been previously undertaken either in Canada, or in other countries. The basic question to be examined is, then, whether foreign-controlled firms claim a profitability premium which can be ascribed to foreign control per se, and not to other factors normally determining inter-firm differences in profitability. In other words, we are asking whether there is a "return to multinationality," the interpretation of which will be discussed in Section V-6. The estimated equations are presented in Section V-3.

The model, as developed here, may also be used to analyse other features of foreign-control in Canada. Section V-4 is devoted to an analysis of differences in the determinants of profitability among the control groups, with specific reference to the extent of foreign ownership (as opposed to control) as a factor determining profitability.

Sections V-3 and V-4 use data averaged over the sample period. However, relative profitability, and its determinants, may change over the course of the business cycle. Section V-5, analyses the role of the business cycle in determining profitability, emphasizing the comparative behaviour of Canadian- and foreign-controlled firms over the cycle.

As a final introductory comment, we note that there is some disagreement over the appropriate measure of profitability to be used in models of the type discussed here. Hall and Weiss argued that the appropriate measure should be the after-tax rate of return on net worth (or assets) since these are expected to equalize when capital markets are working perfectly. This is consistent with their view that inter-firm differences in profitability are the result of structural phenomena, and not efficiency differences. When inter-firm differences in profitability are interpreted as being caused by imperfect market structures, and hence by the ability of some firms to raise prices above competitive levels, the profit margin on sales is also a relevant measure, as firms with market power can use it to augment their margins. Mark-up pricing theories would therefore suggest the use of margins.

If one believes that inter-firm differences in profitability result from efficiency differences among firms, then the appropriate measure of profitability would be a pre-tax rate of return, such as EBIT. As noted, EBIT measures the efficiency with which a firm uses its capital, and its use would be called for in this context.

It is beyond the scope of this study to assess the relative merits of the various possible measures. Rather, the three measures of profitability defined in Chapter IV (EBIT, NPK, GPS) have all been employed as dependent variables in the analysis which follows.

V-2 The Model

Given the dependent (profitability) variables discussed above, we are now in a position to specify the model to be employed. The choice of independent variables is related to theoretical considerations, the availability of data, and the dependent variable used in a particular equation.

The following independent variables will be employed:

(a) *Firm size:* while the interpretation remains contentious, firm size is considered to be an important determinant of profitability. Firm size may be considered either as an indication of market power (or the lack thereof) or of (dis)economies of scale. Firm size is measured by total net assets in 1968 (opening size), when averaged data are employed. Previous results indicated that a log specification is best, usually in parabolic form. This is denoted by OSL (opening size in logs) and OSL^2. The signs of the size terms will clearly depend on which dependent variable is employed. This will be discussed below.

(b) *Concentration:* profitability is influenced by the degree of market power possessed by the firm. Market power is measured by various concentration indices, the prediction being that higher degrees of concentration will result in higher levels of profitability, owing to the possibility of overt or covert collusion, and other advantages based on the mutual recognition of oligopoly power. This study utilizes the Herfindahl Index (HERF) for the three-digit industry to which the firm is classified by Statistics Canada.[3]

(c) *Foreign Control and Ownership:* as we have seen, profitability may be influenced by the country of control of the firm, or by the degree of non-resident ownership. In Chapter I, we examined the Hymer-Caves hypothesis that foreign-controlled firms may have advantages over domestic firms in terms of access to parent technology, parent products and other factors involving sunk costs, all of which may enhance their profitability. These factors may be considered as being internal to the firm and thus not available to other firms, i.e., they are monopolized through internal markets. The firms were therefore classified by country of control and assigned dummy variables for Canadian-controlled (CDA), U.S.-controlled (USA) and Other Foreign-controlled (OF). Foreign control is expected to exert a positive impact on profitability. Firms were also classified by the *degree* of non-resident ownership (NRO), a percentage, in order to ascertain whether increasing foreign ownership exerts any impact on profitability.

(d) *Leverage:* the degree of leverage of the firm (LEV) is defined as non-current liabilities/total assets.[4] Hall and Weiss included a leverage term as a measure of financial risk, higher degrees of leverage implying greater financial risk and, on the assumption of risk aversion, higher profitability. They based their argument on the existence of an optimal leverage ratio, a position contrary to that of Modigliani and Miller (1958) who maintain that the value of a firm is independent of the method of finance. In a Hall-Weiss world, a positive profitability-leverage relationship is expected, while in a Modigliani-Miller world none should exist.

(e) *Variance of Profitability over Time:* the variance of profitability measures business risk (the risk associated with the over-all performance of the firm) and is distinct from financial risk. Greater fluctuations in profitability involve higher levels of business risk, and by the risk premium argument, will imply a positive relationship between profitability and its temporal variance. The temporal variance is denoted by a V before the relevant profitability measure (e.g., VEBIT, VGPS).

(f) *The Capital Turnover Ratio (total net assets/sales):* this variable, denoted by KIT is included for several reasons. As Weiss (1974) points out, it is necessary to include this variable in all equations using profit margins as the dependent variable to correct for differing levels of capital intensity. For profit rates to be equalized, high margin firms should also be more capital intensive, thus suggesting a positive relationship when profit margins are used as the dependent variable. Even so, KIT may also serve a more general function which would dictate that it be included in equations using profit rates as the dependent variable. Lower values of KIT may imply greater efficiency in capital utilization (less excess capacity) which will result in higher profitability, thus suggesting a negative sign. KIT may also be a proxy for capital barriers to entry which would permit monopolistic pricing practices, and a positive sign on KIT. Over-all, the result is indeterminant a priori, particularly when profit rates are the dependent variables.

(g) *Average Annual Rate of Growth of Sales (AGS):* this term measures market (demand) conditions facing the firm. Firms in relatively bouyant markets are expected to experience above average profitability, and thus a positive AGS-profitability relationship is expected.[5]

(h) *Other Variables:* data limitations prevented the use of other variables relating to the firm and its industry. Aside from measures of firm-level diversification (see footnote 3), data for some barriers to entry (product differentiation in particular) and tariffs were not available. These are to some extent accounted for by variables already included. For example, Orr (1974) has shown that concentration and barriers to entry are related in Canada. Thus, HERF may serve as a summary measure of industry structure. In order to partially account for product differentiation we have, following Porter (1974), classified firms by product type (consumer convenience, consumer non-convenience, and producer, denoted by CC, CN, P) and these were entered as dummy variables. As far as the tariff is concerned, its omission may not be serious. Canadian industry studies by Jones et al. (1973) and McFetridge (1973) have shown that it has only a marginal effect on profitability, while Bloch (1974) has shown that it acts in concern with concentration to affect profitability. Nevertheless, in order to account for tariffs and other possible omissions, the thirteen two-digit SIC dummy variables defined in Chapter II were entered into the regression equations.

V-3 Regression Results: All Firms

The model which has been discussed thus far may be summarized in the form in which it is to be estimated:

$$P = a + b_1 OSL + b_2 OSL^2 + b_3 HERF + b_4 CDA + b_5 USA + b_6 LEV + b_7 VP$$
$$+ b_8 AGS + b_9 KIT + \sum_{i=1}^{12} d_i I$$

where all independent variables are as defined in Section V-2, ΣI represents the industry dummy variables and P represents profitability.

This equation (or variants thereof) was estimated by ordinary least squares on various subsets of the sample: averaged data, annual data, and by control group. It is readily apparent that with three possible dependent variables, the number of equations which could be presented is unmanageable. As a consequence, only selected results are reported.

Before proceeding to these results several preliminary observations are in order. In cross-section models of the type employed here, heteroscedasticity, caused by a negative size-within group variance of profitability relationship, is often encountered. In order to discover whether this represented a problem, the absolute value of the residual of each observation in *each* estimated equation was computed and the Spearman rank correlation coefficient was computed between it and the measure of size employed (see Johnston, 1972, p.

219). In no case was a significant relationship discovered and therefore no correction for heteroscedasticity was deemed necessary.

Each equation was also estimated by control group, and covariance analysis was applied to ensure that pooling was warranted (see Johnston, p. 198-202). It was ascertained that no differences in slope existed and that only intercept dummies were required. However, in the case of EBIT, the null hypothesis of similar slopes would have been rejected at 12% significance levels.

Multicollinearity did exist, but in most cases was sufficiently mild as to represent no problem. There was some collinearity amongst financial variables, between size and some financial variables, and between control categories and other variables. [6] In these cases the simple correlation coefficient was less than the estimated $\bar{R}^2$ of the equation in question. In one case, however, the problem was severe. The product type dummies were highly collinear with the industry dummies, as might be expected. As a consequence, the former were not significant and are not reported here.[7] The industry dummies capture all the information provided by the product type dummies, although their interpretation becomes more difficult as product differentiation is no longer distinguishable from the tariff or other factors which are industry specific.

The results for all firms, using averaged data, are presented in Table V-1. Equations 1, 2, and 3 represent the basic model, using the three profitability measures, while equation 4 is a variant, illustrated with EBIT. It can be seen that most of the variables are significant at the 5% level and the explanatory power of the equations, while not high, is satisfactory by cross-section firm data standards. The NPK equation performs less well than the others. This is not unexpected as it will be recalled that NPK has a high standard deviation.

The results are generally consistent with a priori expectations. For EBIT and NPK the best fitting size-profitability specification remains parabolic, with profitability first decreasing and then increasing with size. However, most of the sample firms fall on the downward sloping part of the curve. Only 35 to 45 firms are in the positive size-profitability range, a majority of these being foreign-controlled. Indeed, for EBIT and NPK, size is the most important variable in the equation (as measured by the beta-statistic). GPS, on the other hand, exhibits no significant size-profitability relationship at all. This conclusion remains unaltered when other specifications of the size term are employed. Nevertheless, HERF is strongly and positively related to GPS, while it is positively and less strongly related to EBIT and negatively, but not significantly, related to NPK.

In general, then, concentration appears to exert a positive effect on profitability, and its impact is distinguishable from that of size. As large firms do tend to cluster somewhat in concentrated industries, it is also true that a large firm in a concentrated industry will be more profitable, cet. par.

In the case of EBIT, the fact that for most firms increased size reduces profitability lends credence to the view that size does not simply reflect power to set prices or preclude competition, but also captures the effects of (dis)economies of scale to the firm. This interpretation is reinforced by the fact that EBIT is an efficiency measure. In the case of GPS, where size has no impact but HERF does, we may be observing the classic effects of market power on price. If GPS does indeed represent the planned or ex-ante mark-up, then it should be positively related to HERF, the market power index, but not necessarily to size, the (at least in part) economies of scale index.

U.S.-controlled firms enjoy a premium of 3.5-4.0% on EBIT and 3.3-3.5% on GPS, cet. par. As the constant term represents an Other Foreign firm in the Miscellaneous Industry category, we conclude that U.S.-controlled firms are more profitable than either Canadian- or Other Foreign-controlled firms, cet. par. This conclusion holds only weakly for NPK. The U.S. coefficient is positive, but not significant.[8] However, NPK is inflated for OF firms, and the importance of this equation should be discounted. In equation 4 the control dummies are replaced by the non-resident ownership ratio (NRO) and it is seen that increasing NRO is associated with higher profitability. The same result is encountered when GPS is used to measure profitability. The significance of this result is considered in the concluding section.

There are some sign problems. The variables representing risk (LEV and VP) carry negative signs and are significant. It was argued above that the signs should be positive. These results are not unusual, however. Hall and Weiss found a negative relationship between leverage and profitability, while Shepherd found a negative relationship between profitability and its variation. Gale (1972) attempted to explain the Hall-Weiss result by arguing that low leverage represents not low financial risk, but rather high business risk, given that high business risk firms will find it difficult to borrow, and are thus constrained to low leverage levels. This interpretation has been questioned by Hurdle (1974) and the matter remains unresolved. The negative sign on the variance terms is equally problematical. It could be argued that large firms in concentrated industries achieve both high profitability and low variance by some combination of planning, price-rigidity, tacit collusion, etc. This reasoning is not supported by the data, as no relationship between the variance of profitability and either size or concentration could be found.[9]

TABLE V-1

ALL FIRMS, AVERAGED 1968-1972

Dependent Variables / Independent Variables	(1) EBIT B	SE	(2) GPS B	SE	(3) NPK B	SE	(4) EBIT B	SE
Food and Beverages	−.04*	.01	−.06*	.02	−.03	.02	−.04*	.01
Leather, Textiles, Clothing	−.07*	.02	−.13*	.02	−.08*	.02	−.06*	.02
Wood Products	−.03**	.02	−.13*	.03	−.05*	.02	−.03**	.02
Pulp & Paper	−.05*	.02	−.10*	.02	−.05*	.02	−.05*	.02
Primary Metals	−.08*	.02	−.18*	.02	−.10*	.02	−.08*	.02
Metal Fabricating	−.05*	.01	−.11*	.02	−.07*	.02	−.04*	.02
Machinery	−.06*	.02	−.12*	.02	−.07*	.02	−.06*	.02
Transportation Eq't	−.04*	.01	−.18*	.02	−.04*	.02	−.03*	.01
Electrical Products	−.06*	.01	−.11*	.02	−.05*	.02	−.06*	.02
Non-Metallic Minerals	−.06*	.02	−.07*	.03	−.07*	.03	−.05*	.02
Petroleum	−.04	.03	.00	.03	−.07*	.03	−.06*	.03
Chemicals	−.02	.02	.03**	.02	−.04*	.02	−.02*	.02
USA	.035*	.012	.033*	.012	.012	.011		
CDA	.011	.009	.010	.008	−.000	.019		
NRO							.0002*	.000
OSL	−.114*	.041	−.022	.058	−.126*	.056	−.109*	.041
OSL²	.005*	.002	.000	.003	.006*	.003	.005*	.002
LEV	−.077*	.018	−.084*	.024	−.128*	.024	−.078*	.018
AGS	.030*	.014	.065*	.020	.040*	.020	.023**	.015
HERF	.085*	.038	.115*	.053	−.013	.053	.059**	.038

TABLE V-1 (Cont'd.)

KIT	−.013*	.003	.005	.004	.003	.004	−.013*	.003
VP	−.245*	.030	−.002*	.000	−.192*	.041	−.242*	.030
constant	.085		.227		.114		.782	
R̄²	.24		.33		.15		.26	
F	11.97		19.29		6.13		11.92	
( )	(21,728)		(21,728)		(21,728)		(20,729)	

Notes: * = significant at 5% (one-tailed test)
         ** = significant at 10% (one-tailed test)
         SE = standard error

Another ambiguity arises in the case of KIT, the assets to sales ratio. The previous discussion indicated that both positive and negative signs could be expected. However, the results in Table V-1 indicate that KIT has a negative sign and is significant in the EBIT equation, but has a positive sign, and is not significant in the GPS and NPK equations. The simplest explanation is that the ratio is related to the profitability measures only in a definitional sense, since its numerator is the denominator of EBIT and its denominator is the denominator in the case of GPS. It is also possible that KIT is actually measuring capital efficiency, particularly capacity-utilization, and therefore is related to EBIT, the efficiency index, but not to NPK and GPS. The results do not change when KIT is omitted from the equations.[10]

The industry dummy variables, which by and large are significant, provide an index of relative industry profitability for firms of equal size, leverage etc. For example, if everything else is the same, the EBIT of a Wood Products firm is 4 percentage points higher than a leather, clothing and textile firm. It does not matter that the former is likely to be larger in size than the latter, which would enhance its profitability even more, if it achieved very large size.

Considering EBIT, it is clear that, cet. par., the chemical, wood products, food and beverage, transportation, and petroleum industries are more profitable. Leather, clothing and textiles, and primary metals are the least profitable. GPS provides slightly different results. Chemicals, petroleum, and food and beverages remain high profitability industries, but transportation equipment has a low mark-up, as do the primary metals and leather, clothing and textiles industries.

No matter how one looks at it, the chemical, petroleum, and food and beverage industries are Canada's most profitable; leather, clothing and textiles are, not surprisingly, the least profitable.

These industry dummies clearly indicate that there are inter-industry differences in the level of profitability. The question remains as to the cause of these differences. One explanation might be the tariff. It is often hypothesized that high tariff industries will be high profit industries, since foreign competition is excluded. Only impressionistic evidence can be brought to bear on this issue.

As mentioned, the most profitable industries appear to be food and beverages, petroleum, and chemicals. According to rankings published by the Economic Council of Canada,[11] the petroleum industry ranks 55th in nominal tariffs, but second in effective tariff protection. This seems to confirm the relationship. The other two industries, however, are composed of 3-digit industries which covered a broad range of rankings, none of which seemed unequivocally high. Looking at the matter from the other direction, two low profitability industries are primary metals, which seems to be a medium tariff industry, and the garment related industries which are mostly high (and rising) tariff industries.

Thus, there seems to be no unambiguous relationship between profitability and the tariff.[12] More important, this conclusion must be considered as highly tentative.

The most significant result to come out of this section is that U.S.-controlled firms are more profitable than either Canadian- or Other Foreign-controlled firms when other factors determining inter-firm differences in profitability are held constant. U.S.-controlled firms alone earn a profitability premium above that associated with market power, as traditionally defined, or other factors unique to firms and their industries.

V-4   Regression, Results: Control Groups

In spite of the homogeneity tests, some information can be obtained by considering the control groups separately.[13] Table V-2 presents a version of the model by control group, using EBIT as the dependent variable. EBIT is presented because it exhibits the strongest differences. The broad conclusions outlined below remain unchanged when other dependent variables are considered. The equations include NRO in order to examine the impact of the degree of foreign ownership on profitability.[14] If in fact there is a return to foreign ownership, then profitability and NRO will be positively related. This would suggest a preference for total, or nearly total ownership of subsidiaries. The absence of such a relationship would indicate a preference for joint-ventures or other forms of Canadian participation in ownership. Furthermore, if there is some intrinsic advantage to foreign ownership, then Canadian-controlled firms which have some degree of non-resident ownership may benefit from it.

Table V-2 indicates that NRO is positive and significant (at 10%) for U.S. firms, negative and significant (at 5%) for Other Foreign firms and insignificant for Canadian firms. Foreign participation apparently is not helpful to Canadian-controlled firms, while Canadian participation is helpful to Other Foreign firms, thus suggesting that the latter would be more inclined to seek joint ventures. U.S. firms are likely to continue to own a large share of their subsidiaries, as U.S. ownership seemingly brings with it some intangible advantage. Globerman (1979) has shown that there is an external spill-over effect from foreign ownership in Canadian industries. Canadian-con-

TABLE V-2

The Profitability Model: Regression Equations, by Control Group

Dependent Variables	U.S. EBIT		OF EBIT		CAN EBIT	
Independent Variables	B	SE	B	SE	B	SE
Food & Beverages	.00	.02	−.02	.03	−.06*	.02
Leather, Clothing, Textiles	.00	.03	−.06**	.04	−.11*	.02
Wood Products	−.02	.03	−.04	.05	−.03*	.02
Pulp & Paper	−.02	.03	−.01	.03	−.08*	.02
Primary Metals	−.05**	.03	−.05*	.03	−.11*	.03
Metal Fabricating	.00	.02	−.04	.03	−.08*	.02
Machinery	−.02	.02	−.06*	.03	−.07*	.03
Transport. Eq't.	.03	.02	−.07*	.03	−.09*	.02
Electrical Products	−.01	.02	.03	.03	−.13*	.03
Non-Metallic Minerals	−.02	.04	−.04*	.03	−.08*	.03
Petroleum	−.02	.03	−.02	.03		
Chemicals	−.04*	.02	−.03	.03	.09*	.03
NRO	.0006**	.0004	−.001*	.000	.000	.000
OSL	−.171*	.057	.099	.086	−.003	.006
OSL^2	.008*	.003	.004	.004		
LEV	−.094*	.029	−.104*	.030	−.050**	.029
HERF	.020	.056	.140*	.076	.150*	.063
KIT	−.008**	.005	.003	.004	−.022*	.005
VEBIT	−.159	.350	−1.803	1.116	−.253*	.031
Constant	1.030		.776		.211	
$\bar{R}^2$	.19		.47		.37	
F	4.14		3.60		9.58	
( )	(19,342)		(19,78)		(17,272)	

Notes: See Table V-1.

trolled firms were found to be more productive when faced with foreign competition. This result does not appear to hold for internal spill-overs, in the sense that the presence of minority foreign interests does not enhance the profitability of Canadian-controlled firms.

Table V-2 reveals that there are other differences amongst the control groups.[15] U.S. firms conform to the parabolic size-profitability relationship, and size is the most important determinant of profitability for U.S. firms. HERF is positive, but not significant for these firms. For Canadian-controlled firms the reverse is true. There is no relationship between size and profitability which is significant, and concentration is the most important determinant of profitability. The best fitting size indicator is OSL alone, which bears a negative sign. Thus, for Canadian-controlled firms there is a mild tendency for profitability to decline with size, and no upturn is in evidence. However, this relationship is very weak. Other Foreign firms do conform to the parabolic relationship, but the coefficients are not significant, although the t-values are greater than one. As with the Canadian firms, HERF is a more important determinant of profitability than is size.

It is also true that the industry dummies are insignificant in the case of U.S. firms, are more significant for Other Foreign firms, and almost completely significant for Canadian firms. Hence, industry plays virtually no role in determining profitability for U.S. firms, but is crucial for Canadian-controlled firms. It seems fair to conclude that U.S. firms' profitability is related to firm specific properties such as size, but Canadian firms' profitability is most related to industry characteristics, including concentration. Other Foreign firms lie between these extremes.

NRO is collinear with size. In the cases of U.S. and Other Foreign firms, the relationship is mildly negative; in the case of Canadian firms there is a stronger, positive relationship.[16] The greater the foreign involvement in a Canadian-controlled firm, the larger it tends to be. The exclusion of the NRO term from the U.S. and OF equations does not change things very much, but its exclusion from the CAN equation makes the size-profitability relationship more strongly negative.

U.S. firms may be said to be influenced by *internal* factors, that is, by factors relating to their internal structure and organization. Canadian-controlled firms are influenced by *external* factors, in the sense that their profitability is related to being in a specific industry, or to the possession of monopoly power. Canadian-controlled firms are apparently unable to take advantage of those economies of size which do exist.

The coefficient on the VEBIT term is uniformly negative, but is only significant in the CAN equation. Thus, Canadian-controlled firms, which have the highest profit variability, also exhibit the strongest negative EBIT-VEBIT relationship. Canadian firms are, therefore, in the very strange position of being less profitable than U.S. firms, having more volatile profitability, and the least profitable Canadian-controlled firms have the most volatile profits.

In general terms, the regression results in Table V-2 must be approached with some caution owing to the multicollinearity problem which is greater when the equations are estimated by control groups. However, caution should apply to the values of the estimated coefficients, and not necessarily to the conclusions outlined above. The independent variables were entered into the regression model in different combinations, and many were regressed singly on profitability. While the value of the coefficients did change, depending on the specification, their sign and significance rarely changed.

It is therefore reasonable to conclude that there are some differences in the determinants of profitability by control category, particularly between U.S. and Canadian firms. The former are most influenced by size, the latter by industrial characteristics. For U.S. firms, the negative effects of firm size are partially overcome by advantages to U.S. ownership. Canadian-controlled firms show a strong negative relationship between profitability and its temporal variance.

V-5 Profitability and the Business Cycle

We have thus far considered average profitability over the period 1968-1972. This approach tends, however, to mask year-to-year differences in profitability which are caused by the business cycle. This section will focus on the effects of the business cycle.

The precise effect of the business cycle on firm pricing and profitability is not well established in economic theory. It is sometimes hypothesized that large firms and/or firms in concentrated industries may raise their prices *least* in periods of inflation, for reasons associated with oligopolistic interdependence.[17] The argument proceeds to claim that these firms then tend to make up their relative losses in the downswings, either by raising prices (engaging in counter-cyclical pricing behaviour), or at least by lowering their prices by lesser relative amounts. This leads to the hypothesis that the firm size-concentration-profitability relationship will be strongest in periods of recession, and less strong in periods following the recession.[18] In other words, large firms and/or firms in concentrated industries will achieve relatively higher levels of profitability in recession years. In a profitability model this may be manifested in several ways. One might expect that the magnitude of the size and concentration terms would be higher in a recession year than in the upswing, or more strongly, that the signs of the coefficients could change from year to year. For example, a positive profitability-concentration relationship in a recession year may become negative in the expansion phase.

In order to examine these hypotheses, the two years 1970 and 1971 were selected for further analysis. Certainly, 1970 was a recession year by any indicator, and in 1971 the economy began to move into an expansionary period. The years were chosen for this reason, and because they were concurrent. The profitability model was estimated for each of these years.[19] As explained above, the size-concentration-profitability relationship is expected to hold more strongly in 1970 than in 1971. Furthermore, one expects that this will hold most strongly for GPS, the gross profit margin, which is likely to be related directly to pricing behaviour.

These equations are presented in Table V-3, for all firms.[20] The following broad observations may be made:

(1) The over-all relationship (as indicated by the $\bar{R}^2$) is less successful in explaining the inter-firm differences in profitability in 1971 than in 1970, in the case of both EBIT and GPS. The Chow test confirms that these equations are different from one another in both slope and intercept.

(2) As hypothesized, the coefficient of the Herfindahl Index is not only higher in 1970 than in 1971, but loses significance in 1971 in the EBIT equation. For GPS, however, there is no change in HERF, contrary to the hypothesis.[21]

(3) When size is considered, the results are somewhat ambiguous. According to the EBIT equation, the hypothesis should be rejected since large firms did better in 1971 than in 1970. In 1970 EBIT turned up for only the very largest firms, with assets of about 200 million, whereas in 1971 profitability turned up at a size of about 60 million in assets, other things being held equal. When GPS is considered, there is a problem of interpretation, given that in both years the size coefficients are not significant. However, there is a sign reversal between 1970 and 1971, and it is in the hypothesized direction: profitability turns down for the largest firms in 1971. Nevertheless, this result is very weak.

(4) U.S. firms apparently conform more to the hypothesized behaviour than do Canadian firms. The coefficient for the U.S. dummy is significant for both EBIT and GPS in 1970, but is insignificant in 1971. In 1970 a U.S. firm was likely to have an EBIT which was 4.3%

TABLE V-3

The Profitability Model: For 1970 and 1971, Total Sample

	1970 EBIT		1970 GPS		1971 EBIT		1971 GPS	
	B	SE	B	SE	B	SE	B	SE
Food & Beverages	−.01	.02	−.06*	.02	−.03	.03	−.07*	.02
Leather, Clothing, Textiles	−.07*	.02	−.13*	.02	−.08*	.03	−.13*	.02
Wood Products	−.12*	.02	−.21*	.03	−.09*	.04	−.13*	.03
Pulp & Paper	−.03	.02	−.09*	.02	−.12*	.03	−.10*	.02
Primary Metals	−.07*	.02	−.18*	.03	−.10*	.03	−.19*	.03
Metal Fabricating	−.04*	.02	−.11*	.02	−.04*	.03	−.11*	.02
Machinery	−.05*	.02	−.12*	.02	−.07*	.03	−.12*	.02
Transport. Eq't.	−.05*	.02	−.20*	.02	−.05**	.03	−.18*	.02
Electrical Products	−.06*	.02	−.12*	.02	−.08*	.03	−.10*	.02
Non-Metallic Minerals	−.07*	.02	−.05**	.03	−.07***	.04	−.05**	.03
Petroleum	−.04	.03	.03	.04	−.09*	.05	.00	.04
Chemicals	−.01	.02	.04*	.02	−.02	.03	.02	.02
U.S.A.	.043*	.013	.032*	.015	.027	.021	.010	.015
CDA	.014	.013	.017	.016	−.014	.022	−.019	.016
Size (logs)	−.099*	.050	−.020	.061	−.176*	.084	.004	.061
Size² (logs)	.004*	.002	.001	.003	.008*	.004	−.000	.003
HERF	.125*	.046	.125*	.055	.076	.075	.125*	.056
LEVERAGE	−.092*	.021	−.071*	.025	−.093*	.034	−.089*	.025

TABLE V-3 (Cont'd.)

Constant	.685	.429	1.091	.322
$\bar{R}^2$	.148	.255	.093	.211
F	7.04	13.87	3.959	10.76
( )	(18,736)	(18,731)	(18,731)	(18,731)

Notes: See Table V-1.

higher than either an Other Foreign or Canadian firm, *cet. par.* In 1971 there was unlikely to be any difference amongst the control groups.

When we consider all of these factors together, it seems that there is only limited evidence to support the hypothesis that monopoly elements in the economy behave differently over the business cycle. The effect of industrial concentration has been found to be greater in the down year of the sample period only for EBIT. Larger firms do not seem to behave counter-cyclically. However, if the large firm is in a concentrated industry, which is by and large the case, then one has more confidence in affirming the hypothesis.[22] If, in addition, the firm is U.S. controlled, then it is very likely that the firm will be more profitable in the recession year, relative to other firms.

In order to reduce the ambiguity of the behaviour of GPS with respect to firm size, an additional test was undertaken. The radio GPS_t/GPS_{t-1}, where t is the year, was defined for the years 1969-1970 and 1970-1971. The former period was one of declining economic activity, and the latter was when the recovery began. The hypothesis is that large firms will be more successful in protecting their margins on the downswing, and will then accept lesser margin increases on the upswing.[23]

The GPS ratio for each of the two periods was therefore regressed on OSL and the control dummies. The results are as follows:

$$\text{GPS70/GPS69} \quad 2.428 - .158\ \text{OSL} + .125\ \text{USA} - .131\ \text{CDA} \quad \bar{R}^2 = .019$$
$$\phantom{\text{GPS70/GPS69} \quad 2.428}\ (.107)\phantom{\ \text{OSL} + }(.339)\phantom{\ \text{USA} - }(.352)$$
$$\text{GPS71/GPS70} - 1.156 + .251^{**}\ \text{OSL} - .440\ \text{USA} + .040\ \text{CDA} \quad \bar{R}^2 = .030$$
$$\phantom{\text{GPS71/GPS70} - 1.156}\ (.138)\phantom{ + .251^{**}}(.437)\phantom{\ \text{USA} + }(.454)$$

Turning first to the equation for GPS 70/GPS 69, we see that the coefficient of the size term is negative, meaning that firms of above average size experienced below average margin changes between 1969 and 1970. This relationship is not significant, but comes close. Thus, the first part of the hypothesis is confirmed, but weakly.

Over the years 1970-71, however, this was reversed. The coefficient of the size term becomes positive and is significant at 10% on a two-tailed test, and at 5% on a one-tailed test. Firms which were above average in size experienced above average changes in profit margins. This is contrary to the second part of the hypothesis, and does not correspond to the findings of Dennis, mentioned in footnote 23.

Included in the equations are the control dummies. They are not significant, but do exhibit an interesting sign reversal. Canadian-controlled firms follow the hypothesized behaviour more on the downswing than on the upswing. The reverse is true of U.S.-controlled firms. U.S. firms are least likely to reduce their margins on the downswing and least likely to increase them on the upswing. This result, while not significant, is consistent with the fact that U.S. firms do exhibit a more stable temporal variance of profitability. Apparently, then, U.S. firms are unlikely to see their profit margins change over the business cycle, while Canadian-controlled firms will experience substantial fluctuation. This cannot be considered a strong conclusion, but is certainly a tendency which deserves further research.

V-6 Summary and Conclusions

This chapter has analysed the profitability of Canadian- and foreign-controlled firms within the context of a general model designed to explain inter-firm differences in profitability. Thus, in addition to generating results specific to the subject of foreign control, the model has also produced more general results. We begin by summarizing the latter.

Generally speaking, the profitability model presented here compares favourably with its U.S. antecedents. The degree of explanatory power of the equations is adequate by the standards of such models, but it remains true that a large percentage of inter-firm profitability differences remain unexplained. It is also true that some aspects of the results remain unexplained, such as the negative relationship between profitability and measures of risk. The use of several measures of profitability as dependent variables revealed that the results differ somewhat according to the measure employed. The differences are most pronounced when firm size and concentration are considered. Profit margins are unrelated to firm size, but are highly related to concentration; profit rates are more related to firm size, but are also related to concentration. The results were found to differ very little when profit rates were measured, before or after taxes.

Of primary interest, however, are the results specific to foreign ownership and control, and their interpretation. It has been found that U.S.-controlled firms are more profitable than either Canadian- or Other Foreign-controlled firms, when other factors are held constant. In addition, the more profitable U.S. controled firms are, the higher is the degree of non-resident (presumably American) ownership. The same is not true of Other Foreign firms; their profitability declines with the degree of non-resident ownership. The profitability of Canadian-controlled is unaffected by the degree of foreign participation.

It is abundantly clear that U.S.-controlled firms possess a profitability advantage above and beyond that associated with market power, as it is traditionally measured. The evidence suggests that this advantage is internal to the firm, and increases with the amount of control exercised from abroad. For U.S. firms, these results are consistent with the Hymer-Caves approach to multinationals. U.S.-controlled firms apparently possess some advantage which is best exploited within the firm itself and which cannot be transferred to other firms, but which can be transferred within the global firm. U.S.-controlled firms are not likely, therefore, to seek or encourage Canadian participation.

The same conclusions cannot be drawn in the case of Other Foreign firms. They possess no profitability advantage and tight foreign control does not enhance profitability. Either the Hymer-Caves hypothesis cannot claim general validity, or the Other Foreign firms do not possess, or have yet to assert, those characteristics associated with true MNCs. In other words, if our results are meaningful, the implication is that either advantages of multinationality are in fact advantages of nationality, specifically U.S.-nationality; or that non-U.S. firms in Canada are, as a group, recent arrivals in the Canadian economy and have not yet established themselves in their new environment. Such firms may be receptive to joint ventures or other forms of Canadian participation.

With respect to Canadian-controlled firms, our results indicate that when such a firm is above average in profitability, it is the result of being in a profitable industry, or of possessing some monopoly power. However, a U.S.-controlled firm in the same industry, and with the same degree of monopoly power would be yet more profitable. Foreign participation in the ownership of Canadian-controlled firms does not enhance their profitability. Minority foreign ownership of Canadian-controlled firms is apparently a portfolio investment which does not bring with it a transfer of knowledge, skills or techniques.

While the statistical results summarized above are unambiguous, their interpretation for policy purposes is. How does one interpret the profitability advantage possessed by U.S.-controlled firms? The Hymer-Caves approach suggests that the advantage originates in the monopolization of an asset which is best allocated internally, rather than through external markets. If this interpretation is accepted, the conclusion would be that U.S.-controlled firms are earning monopoly profits as a result of market imperfections. The market imperfections may be interpreted as a barrier to entry in the form of closed access to technology, products, or funds. In such a case the appropriate policy would call for public intervention in the form of subsidies to Canadian-controlled firms for technology and product development and/or restrictions on U.S.-controlled firms in the form of taxes, regulations to encourage technology diffusion, or other forms of regulation. However, one cannot rule out the possibility that U.S.-controlled firms are simply more efficient, particularly in management. The evidence presented in Chapter III suggested that U.S.-controlled firms are not more efficient in utilizing current assets, particularly inventories, but they are more efficient in utilizing total assets. The latter is accounted for in the regression equations and is thus not the source of the profitability advantage. Nevertheless, U.S.-controlled firms may possess some organizational advantages which account for the difference. If this is so, then no public policy is called for so long as the policy-makers are willing to accept the continued control of resources by foreign-controlled firms.

The determinants of profitability have been found to change over the course of the business cycle, particularly where U.S.-controlled firms are concerned. The U.S. profitability advantage is highest in periods of recession, and disappears, or at least is eroded, in the expansion phase. This result is consistent with counter-cyclical pricing behaviour on the part of U.S. firms, and helps to explain the relative stability of their profits over time. Only weak evidence was found to support suggestions that firms with market power engage in counter-cyclical pricing. An important implication of this result is that any controls programme which freezes a profit structure into place during a period of recession will discriminate against Canadian-controlled firms, and possibly against small firms, depending on how profits are controlled.

The evidence weighs heavily towards the interpretation that the firm size-profitability relationship measures efficiency in some broad sense. Profit rates decline with size up to the largest firms, while margins are unaffected by size. The upturn in profit rates at large size is, for the most part, restricted to foreign-controlled firms. It cannot be argued that as size increases firms tend to sacrifice profits for security, since there is no relationship between firm size and profit variability. It might be argued, however, that as size increases firms are led away from profit maximizing behaviour, perhaps owing to organizational slack. It could also be argued that firms gain market power from large size, although this would imply that there is a size threshold beyond which such power is exercised.

If one accepts the view that the very largest firms are more efficient, and adopts policies to encourage their formation, the result would likely be an increase in foreign ownership.

Notes

1. Industry studies are reviewed by Weiss (1974). Canadian studies using this methodology are by McFetridge (1973) and Jones et al. (1973).

2. The seminal paper on inter-firm differences in profitability was by Hall and Weiss (1967). The methodology has been refined by the addition of more explanatory variables. See Shepherd (1972) and Carter (1977).

3. This procedure fails to capture the market power possessed by firms operating in other than their primary 3-digit industry. No data were available on the degree of diversification by firm, and no adjustment could be made. The 4 and 8 firm concentration ratios were also used to classify industries according to the level of concentration, but the reported results do not change as a result of their use.

4. Other leverage measures such as LEVT, which was defined in Chapter III, were also employed, but no change in the reported results occurred as a consequence of this substitution.

5. This variable is included by Shepherd (1972) and implies that growth causes profitability. Marris (whose argument is summarized by Eatwell, 1971), argues that the causality is reversed. We include this variable, not only in appealing to historical precedent, but also because a legitimate distinction can be made between the growth of sales as an index of market conditions, and the growth of assets as an index of discretionary firm growth.

6. There was also an absence of a multicollinearity in some cases where it might have been expected, e.g., between U.S. (dummy) and HERF, and between size and the variance of profitability.

7. When entering the equation without the industry dummies, CC and CN were both positive and significant, i.e., consumer goods industries were more profitable than producer goods industries.

8. However, the t-statistic is 1, lending some importance to the result.

9. Selected simple correlation coefficients are $r_{OSL, VEBIT} = -.005$; $r_{OSL, VGPS} = .028$; $r_{HERF, VEBIT} = .003$; $r_{HERF, VGPS} = .029$. It should be noted that while large firms tend to more highly levered, concentration and leverage are not related.

10. The same result is found when fixed assets alone replace total assets in the numerator. When percentage labour costs (ULP or ULT) are used as a measure of capital intensity (in fact, its inverse), there is an unambiguous and strong negative relationship between these and any measure of profitability. Firms with above average profitability are those with below average labour costs. It could be argued that high labour cost firms employ more labour because labour is relatively unproductive. Low labour productivity may in turn be caused by low capital intensity. Thus, the negative labour-cost-profitability relationship is explained by differences in capital intensity. High capital intensity in this interpretation is unambiguously related to high profitability.

11. Economic Council of Canada, *Looking Outward*, Information Canada,

Ottawa 1975, Table 8-1. The rankings include 97 mining and manufacturing industries.

12. See Bloch (1974) for a discussion of this matter.

13. While the test for homogeneity (the Chow-test) revealed that no differences in slopes existed among the control groups, such tests are based on *all* regression coefficients and could mask differences in specific coefficients.

14. It will be recalled that NRO, the non-resident ownership ratio, is a percentage reflecting the degree to which a firm is owned by non-residents. It does not imply control. The latter required (in general) an NRO of more than 50%.

15. These results hold only for EBIT.

16. The simple correlation coefficients between OSL and NRO are:

$$
\begin{array}{ll}
\text{U.S.:} & -.109 \\
\text{OF:} & -.128 \\
\text{CAN:} & .298
\end{array}
$$

17. This argument is concisely summarized by Weiss (1974).

18. See Weiss, op. cit. p. 200. Weiss suggests that large size confers market power, an interpretation which, as noted, may be incorrect.

19. The model was also estimated for the other years, but the "strongest" results were obtained for 70-71, as expected. However, the dummy variable for U.S.-controlled firms, which will be shown to be insignificant in 1971, reverted to a positive and significant sign in 1972, although its magnitude was not as great as in 1970.

20. Those terms which are related to the period as a whole (AGS, VEBIT, VGPS) have been omitted for obvious reasons. The NPK equation is omitted as it followed the pattern of EBIT.

21. When the above equations were estimated using the net profit margin, it was found that the HERF coefficient did change signs, from positive in 1970 to negative in 1971. In neither case was the coefficient significant, although the t-value exceeded one.

22. It can be shown that large firms' EBIT increased more over 1970-1971 than did that of small firms, if all other factors are considered equal. However, when different values of HERF are assigned to large and small firms, and given that HERF becomes insignificant in 1971, it can be shown that the differential increase becomes very small.

23. Dennis (1973), in a study prepared for the Prices and Incomes Commission, found that on an industry basis, changes in the ISPI were most negatively related with firm size on the upswing.

VI

GROWTH

VI-1 Introduction

We now turn to the second of the performance indicators defined in this study: firm growth. The study of firm growth is important for a number of reasons. At the macro-economic level, it is clear that the growth of firms is related to the growth of the economy, and thereby to employment creation. At the micro-economic level, the growth process of firms is relevant to the process of aggregate and industrial concentration. It is intuitively obvious that if large firms grow faster than small firms, then the share of output produced by large firms, and hence aggregate concentration, will increase, other factors being held constant. While the results presented here will have some relevance to these concerns, it is within the context of foreign control that we will analyse the growth process.

Specifically, this chapter will compare the level and patterns of growth rates of foreign- and Canadian-controlled firms. We have already confirmed that U.S.-controlled firms are more profitable than other firms and should profitability and growth be positively related (as is often the case), then one expects U.S.-controlled firms to grow faster. This would imply that, other things being equal, the share of output controlled by U.S. firms would increase over time. Nonetheless, other factors considered in Chapter I suggested that both the level and pattern of growth of subsidiaries of MNCs might differ from those of domestic firms. It was suggested that the growth of foreign subsidiaries might be less dependent on expansion in a single national market and might therefore be truncated. Furthermore, the entire process of growth of such firms might be controlled from abroad leading to a different growth path.

These are the general considerations which motivate the subsequent analysis. Section VI-2 will define the growth rates to be considered, and will compare the growth performance of foreign- and Canadian-controlled firms. Section VI-3 provides a framework for studying inter-firm differences in growth rates and this framework is employed in Section VI-4. The relationship between profitability and growth is studied in Section VI-5, while VI-6 is devoted to miscellaneous topics relevant to the growth of firms.

VI-2 Measures of Growth

Firm growth may be measured in several ways, the choice often being dependent on the purpose of the analysis. The two most commonly employed growth rates are the growth of sales and the growth of assets. The former is likely to be more related to the market circumstances facing the firm while the latter may be more dependent on the attitude of the firm towards growth, although this distinction is not always clear-cut. Both of these variables will be employed in the subsequent analysis. As noted in Table VI-1, they will be denoted as AGS and AGA, respectively. While these measures are the most widely utilized, and will be accorded the most attention, another measure which has some relevance is the growth of fixed assets (AGFA). AGFA measures the rate at which a firm is augmenting its productive capacity.[1] All growth rates are calculated as average annual proportionate rates of growth.

The growth rates, by country of control, are found in Table VI-2. Before considering these figures, we note that the various growth rates are related. The simple correlation coefficients, all of which are significant at 5%, are as follows: $r_{AGS, AGA} = .33$; $r_{AGA, AGFA} = .48$; $r_{AGS, AGFA} = .18$. As one might expect, the asset-based growth measures are the most highly correlated, and this is reflected in the subsequent empirical results.

It can be seen that the results differ according to the measure under consideration. Foreign-controlled firms grew fastest when AGS and AGFA are considered, while Canadian-controlled firms grew fastest according to AGA. However, the standard deviations are relatively high and as a result, the analyses of variance failed to uncover any significant differences among the growth rates, except in the case of AGFA where Other Foreign-controlled firms were found to grow significantly faster than Canadian-controlled firms.

The interpretation of these results will await their confirmation through regression analysis when other factors influencing firm

TABLE VI-1

GROWTH VARIABLES: DEFINITIONS*

Variable	Symbol	Calculation
Growth of Sales	AGS	$(\text{Log } 39_{72} - \text{Log } 39_{68})/4$
Growth of Assets	AGA	$(\text{Log } 13_{72} - \text{Log } 13_{68})/4$
Growth of Fixed Assets	AGFA	$(\text{Log } 8_{72} - \text{Log } 8_{68})/4$

* Numbers refer to those in the Appendix to Chapter II. All growth rates are proportionate (averaged) over the sample period.

TABLE VI-2

GROWTH RATES: MEANS, BY CONTROL GROUP

Variable	Country of Control	m (%)	s (%)
AGS	U.S.	7.6	16.0
	OF	10.5	37.4
	CAN	6.8	23.9
	TOTAL	7.7	22.8
AGA	U.S.	6.1	9.4
	OF	6.0	11.0
	CAN	7.1	11.3
	TOTAL	6.5	10.4
AGFA	U.S.	4.5	18.4
	OF	7.1^3	33.9
	CAN	3.0^2	33.3
	TOTAL	4.2	27.2

Notes: See Table IV-2.

growth are held constant. The next section will discuss the methodology appropriate to such an analysis.

VI-3 Size and Growth: Theory

It is observed that the size distribution of firms and plants in most countries is skewed, there being many more small firms than large firms. While this is not remarkable, it is true that such skewed distributions are often of a particular type, known as log-normal.[2]

This means that if we measure the size of the firm on one axis, and the frequency distribution of firms by size class on the other axis, and plot them on log paper, the resulting relationship will take the form of a straight line. This relationship is found to be remarkably common amongst countries, not only with respect to the size distribution of firms, but also with respect to the size distribution of cities.

Economic theory is unable to account for this fact. The theory of the firm predicts that all firms will tend towards some optimal size, and that this size will be the same for all firms in the same circumstances. Since this is rarely the case, other explanations have been sought to explain the observed distribution of firms. It was found that the log normal distribution could be generated by certain stochastic processes, one of which has gained particular prominence among economists. This is known as *Gibrat's Law,* or the *law of proportionate effect,* and it states that the chance of changing sizes (growing) is a stochastic phenomenon depending on the mutual interaction of many independent forces. In other words, growth is random in that no firm has a better chance of growing than does any other firm.

It should be understood that random is used here in its statistical sense. Thus, the law does not state that there are no systematic effects governing the growth of firms, but rather that there are so many of them, interacting in so many different directions, that the subsequent effect appears to be random. Therefore, a small firm has as much chance of achieving high rates of growth as does a large firm and in general, all firms, regardless of size, should tend to grow at the same rate over sufficiently long periods of time.

The implications of this *law* are important. If all firms grow at the same rate, the implication is that there is no optimum size for the firm, i.e., the long-run average cost curve is flat (after some point, perhaps). If large firms grow faster than small firms, the implication is that the long-run average cost curve declines continuously. In both cases there is no barrier to the growth of firms. If small firms tend to grow faster than large firms, other things equal, this may be taken as evidence that there is an optimum firm size.

Another implication is that if all firms do grow at the same rate on average, there will be a tendency towards increased concentration so long as there is a dispersion of growth rates around the mean. Intuitively, this is so because large firms can grow bigger or smaller, while small firms can grow bigger, but if they grow smaller, they will disappear. Thus, the output share of large firms increases. This is not a necessary outcome, because it depends on the dispersion of growth rates by size group.[3]

While Gibrat's Law has not always been found to hold, it does provide a convenient framework for analysing the growth process of firms. This framework has been developed in the context of the multinational firm by Rowthorn and Hymer (1971). The next few paragraphs follow their approach.

The *law* may be stated algebraically in the following manner:

(6.1) $S_t/S_{t-1} = e_t$

where S = the size of the firm, t = time, and e = a random variable whose distribution is independent of S_{t-1}.

In words, the ratio of today's size to yesterday's size, which is the growth of the firm, is random. It does not depend on yesterday's size.

Taking logs, and letting $u_t = \log e_t$, we can write,

(6.2) $\log S_t = \log S_{t-1} + u_t$

and therefore,

(6.3) $\log S_t = \log S_0 + u_t + u_{t-1} \ldots + u_1,$

where S_0 is the opening size of the firm.

By the Central Limit Theorem, we may then write,

(6.4) $\log S_t = \log S_0 + v_t.$

This provides us with one statistical test of the Law. We can estimate the equation,

(6.5) $\log S_t = a + b \log S_0 + v_t$

and if b = 1, then the law is confirmed. If, however, b $\neq$ 1, then it implies that growth is not proportionate. If b exceeds 1, then large firms are growing faster than small firms. If b is less than 1, the reverse is true. b < 1 implies a regression towards the mean, and is analagous to the analysis of profitability in Chapter IV. It should be pointed out that b $\geq$ 1 always implies that aggregate concentration will increase, i.e., the output or asset share of the largest firms will increase over time. b < 1 implies, but does not guarantee that concentration will decline.[4] Since the largest firms in the sample are mostly foreign-controlled, the magnitude of b will also be relevant to future trends in foreign ownership.

A more straightforward method, and the one adopted by Rowthorn and Hymer, is to estimate an equation such as,

(6.6) $\quad g = f(S) + u$

where g is the growth rate of the firm, f(S) is a size term(s), and u is an error term.

Specifically, this might take the form,

(6.7) $\quad g = a + b_1 S + b_2 S^2 + e$

where S may be in natural units or logs.

The null hypothesis is that growth and size are unrelated, and therefore that $b_1, b_2 = 0$.

These equations do not account for the industry or control category of the firm, that is, its specific circumstances. This omission may be corrected by the inclusion of the industry and control dummies. Thus,

(6.8) $\quad g = a + b_1 S + b_2 S^2 + \sum_{i=1}^{2} c_i C + \sum_{j=1}^{12} d_j I + e$

where C and I are the control and industry dummies.

The null hypothesis is that once certain systematic effects are eliminated (industry, control group), there will be no relation between size and growth ($b_1, b_2 = 0$). Equation (6.8) is not problem-free as there are almost certainly some variables excluded from it which do exert a systematic influence on firm growth. To the extent that these excluded variables are not correlated with included variables, then the estimated coefficients will be unbiased. The most obvious excluded variable is profitability, a variable which will be considered in Section VI-5. For the moment, it is excluded from the estimated equations, since it is certainly collinear with size. We now turn to the results obtained by estimating equations such as (6.5) and (6.8).

VI-4 Size and Growth: Results

Before presenting the results of the regression analysis, some definitions are in order. Throughout this section, size refers to opening size, unless otherwise mentioned, as measured by assets in 1968. Closing size will refer to assets in 1972.

All three measures of growth have been employed in regression equations of the form suggested by equation (6.8). Nevertheless,

TABLE VI-3

GROWTH RATES, BY SIZE AND CONTROL GROUPS

Size Class (000,000)	Sales				Assets			
	U.S.	OF	CAN	TOT	U.S.	OF	CAN	TOT
1. <5	17.8(17.8)	X	12.1(7.7)	14.9(14.3)	17.4(12.6)	X	16.3(11.9)	16.8(11.8)
2. 5-10	7.9(14.0)	4.6(8.9)	9.0(15.8)	8.1(14.4)	6.3(9.4)	4.8(11.2)	6.8(10.5)	6.4(10.0)
3. 10-20	6.8(21.1)	12.9(13.2)	4.6(26.1)	6.9(22.2)	4.3(8.5)	2.1(7.5)	8.0(10.3)	6.1(9.2)
4. 20-40	5.6(12.8)	12.0(27.2)	.1(48.1)	5.6(31.6)	5.2(9.2)	8.6(16.2)	4.2(16.7)	5.3(13.2)
5. 40-80	6.5(14.8)	13.7(80.5)	7.3(13.6)	8.5(40.5)	7.5(9.4)	4.1(12.1)	7.7(9.7)	6.8(10.2)
6. 80-160	4.1(10.5)	6.7(7.1)	4.8(14.2)	4.8(11.6)	3.2(5.2)	3.1(8.9)	7.0(8.2)	4.7(7.3)
7. >160	10.5(7.9)	4.0(4.7)	8.7(10.9)	9.1(8.9)	3.9(3.9)	6.5(5.6)	2.9(3.4)	3.8(3.9)
TOTAL	7.7(15.7)	10.6(37.4)	6.8(23.9)	7.7(22.8)	6.2(9.4)	6.0(11.0)	7.2(11.3)	6.5(10.4)

Notes: X: omitted to preserve confidentiality
Growth rates are in percentage terms. Figures in parentheses are standard deviations.

TABLE VI-3 (Cont'd.)

Size Class (000,000)	Fixed Assets				Number of Firms			
	U.S.	OF	CAN	TOT	U.S.	OF	CAN	TOT
1. <5	16.5(24.0)	X	16.9(19.4)	15.8(21.8)	20	2	15	37
2. 5-10	3.7(16.5)	2.3(40.0)	1.0(36.4)	2.4(29.0)	137	26	123	286
3. 10-20	2.0(23.3)	3.8(9.4)	4.5(34.1)	3.2(26.4)	78	25	61	164
4. 20-40	4.9(12.6)	5.6(13.6)	1.0(44.1)	3.0(22.8)	53	15	36	104
5. 40-80	6.7(10.7)	2.1(34.3)	5.2(12.1)	5.2(19.2)	37	19	24	80
6. 80-160	3.2(7.1)	2.7(6.3)	6.5(14.3)	4.5(10.5)	19	7	18	44
7. >160	3.8(8.6)	25.5(40.0)	.3(.1)	4.9(15.8)	18	4	13	32
TOTAL	4.5(17.3)	5.4(22.5)	2.6(33.1)	3.4(25.8)	362	98	290	750

these variables may not lend themselves to similar interpretations. As was previously noted, AGS is most related to the market circumstances facing the firm; AGA and AGFA, however, are more likely to reflect the planned expansion of the firm. In other words, AGS may be interpreted as the ability of the firm to grow, while AGA and AGFA are indicators of its willingness to grow. Both sales and asset based growth variables are somewhat biased. The former is susceptible to market conditions, including the differential impact of inflation and capacity utilization. The latter will possibly exaggerate the growth extremes, if slow growth firms possess older assets which are evaluated at lower historical costs. Slow growth firms will therefore appear to grow even more slowly, and vice-versa. There is no precise way of choosing which variable is best, and so we will examine them all.

Table VI-3 presents the relevant growth rates by size and ownership groups. The data are difficult to interpret as no clear pattern of growth emerges either for size or control groups or for some combination of the two. It should be noted that the standard deviations are quite large, and remain so when growth rates are calculated by industry. U.S.-controlled firms appear to have the lowest standard deviations, as do the largest firms, according to all measures.

In order to avoid some of the problems associated with large standard deviations, the Spearman rank correlation coefficients were computed for the size-growth relationships. They are reported in Table VI-4.[5]

Table VI-4 indicates a definite, but weak, negative association between the growth of sales or assets and the size of the firm. There is apparently no relationship between firm size and the growth of fixed assets. This pattern holds true for Canadian- and U.S.-controlled firms, but not for Other Foreign firms.

These results are further analysed by regression analysis in Table VI-5. These equations conform to equation (6.5) as derived in the previous section, and take the following form:

Log Closing Size = a + b Log Opening Size,

where size is measured in both assets and sales. It will be recalled that the magnitude of the estimated b determines whether a process of concentration or regression is occurring. It should also be recalled that the estimation is not based on a full sample of manufacturing firms, and that the sample employed largely excludes mergers. As a consequence, the results cannot be generalized beyond this sample, at least in terms of trends in concentration.

Table VI-5 also presents the reverse equation,

TABLE VI-4

SPEARMAN RANK CORRELATION COEFFICIENTS: SIZE AND GROWTH

OPENING SIZE AND

	GROWTH OF SALES	*GROWTH OF ASSETS*	*GROWTH OF FIXED ASSETS*
Total	$-.085^*$	$-.118^*$	.002
U.S.	$-.116^*$	$-.119^*$	.008
OF	.091	$-.068$	.082
CAN	$-.120^*$	$-.121^*$	$-.016$

Notes: * = significant at 5%

Log Opening Size = a + b Log Closing Size.

This follows the suggestion by Prais (1958) that the first equation is not unambiguous in terms of its interpretation. Only if the estimated b from both equations is less than one (or greater than one), can one make unambiguous statements about the process of concentration or deconcentration.

There is a possibility of heteroscedasticity in these equations which might cause one to reject the hypothesis that b = 1 when in fact it should be accepted. In other words, if the estimated standard errors are too low, then the wrong confidence intervals will result. No evidence of heteroscedasticity was found, and the estimates may thus be taken as minimum variance estimates.

The estimated equations indicate that there is an unambiguous tendency for growth rates to regress towards the mean, as all coefficients are less than 1. The estimated coefficients are all significant and the over-all relationships are strong, except in the case of the OF sales equation. Furthermore, the growth of sales exhibits a far stronger tendency towards regression than does the growth of assets.

The strong tendency towards regression which is found when size is measured in sales is at least partially caused by the extremely low values calculated for Other Foreign Firms. When the assets equations were subjected to homogeneity tests, it was found that the control groups did not differ either by slope or intercept. In this case it may be concluded that the underlying growth process is the same for all firms, and that there is a tendency towards regression to the same mean. This would further imply a decrease in foreign ownership over time, other things being equal.[6] However, when the same tests were performed on the sales equations, it was found that the Other Foreign firms' equations were different in both slope and intercept. U.S.- and Canadian-controlled firms were found not to differ from each other in either slope or intercept. The OF sales equation, it should be noted, has a low degree of explanatory power relative to

TABLE VI-5

Regression: The Relationship Between Opening-Closing Size (Logs)

Total Sample

Dependent Variable	= a +	b_1	Independent Variable	$\bar{R}^2$	F( )
(1) Log Assets (1972)	.838	.940* (.013)	Log Assets (1968)	.87	5138(1,748)
(2) Log Assets (1968)	.446	.929* (.013)	Log Assets (1972)	.87	5138(1,748)
(3) Log Sales (1972)	2.405	.783* (.024)	Log Sales (1968)	.58	1037(1,748)
(4) Log Sales (1968)	2.256	.742* (.023)	Log Sales (1972)	.58	1037(1,748)
		U.S. Firms			
(1) Log Assets (1972)	.748	.948* (.017)	Log Assets (1968)	.90	3098(1,360)
(2) Log Assets (1968)	.297	.945* (.017)	Log Assets (1972)	.90	3098(1,360)
(3) Log Sales (1972)	1.596	.868* (.027)	Log Sales (1968)	.74	1039(1,360)
(4) Log Sales (1968)	1.154	.855* (.026)	Log Sales (1972)	.74	1039(1,360)
		OF Firms			
(1) Log Assets (1972)	.682	.955* (.040)	Log Assets (1968)	.85	563(1,96)
(2) Log Assets (1968)	.830	.894* (.037)	Log Assets (1972)	.85	563(1,96)
(3) Log Sales (1972)	7.848	.229* (.079)	Log Sales (1968)	.08	8.61(1,96)
(4) Log Sales (1968)	6.015	.360* (.122)	Log Sales (1972)	.08	8.61(1,96)
		Can Firms			
(1) Log Assets (1972)	.984	.927* (.023)	Log Assets (1968)	.85	1614(1,288)
(2) Log Assets (1968)	.545	.915* (.023)	Log Assets (1972)	.85	1614(1,288)
(3) Log Sales (1972)	1.442	.876* (.039)	Log Sales (1968)	.63	491(1,288)
(4) Log Sales (1968)	2.462	.719* (.032)	Log Sales (1972)	.63	491(1,288)

Notes: * = significant at 5%

the other equations, suggesting considerable variation in growth rates amongst Other Foreign firms.

The size-growth relationship was also tested directly by regressing the growth rates on size terms. The results for all firms, are reported in Table VI-6. Equations (1) to (3) regress growth on the log of opening size. It can be seen that the relation is found to be negative in all cases, but significant only in the case of AGA. Even so, these are not the best fitting equations. Equations (4) to (6) include the square of the size term (in logs), and it can be seen that these equations provide a better fit. Like the size-profitability relationship, the

TABLE VI-6

**Size and Growth: Selected Regression Equations,
Total Sample**

(1) AGA   .169 − .011* OSL $\bar{R}^2 = .013$; $F(1,748) = 13.40$
          (.003)

(2) AGS   .132 − .006 OSL $\bar{R}^2 = .001$; $F(1,748) = .00$
          (.007)

(3) AGFA .058 − .002 OSL $\bar{R}^2 = .000$; $F(1,748) = .00$
          (.058)

(4) AGA   .829 − .140* OSL + .006* OSL^2 $\bar{R}^2 = .024$; $F(2,747) = 9.33$
          (.045)   (.002)

(5) AGS   1.136 − .203* OSL + .009** OSL^2 $\bar{R}^2 = .006$; $F(2,747) = 2.23$
          (.100)   (.005)

(6) AGFA 1.042 − .195** + .009** OSL^2 $\bar{R}^2 = .004$; $F(2,747) = 1.48$
          (.114)   (.005)

(7) AGA   −1.636* OSL−W + .132* OSL^2−W + 7.711*−W
(Weighted)   (2.34)   (.020)   (1.069)
                                                       $\bar{R}^2 = .160$; $F(3,746) = 45.78$

(8) AGS   −.484* OSL−W + .045* OSL^2−W + 3.234*−W
(Weighted)   (2.30)   (.017)   (3.289)
                                                       $\bar{R}^2 = .017$; $F(3,746) = 4.47$

(9) AGFA   −1.959* OSL−W + .198* OSL^2−W + 11.443* W
(Weighted)   (.582)   (.065)   (3.469)
                                                       $\bar{R}^2 = .024$; $F(3,746) = 6.25$

(10) AGA   .808 − .135* OSL + .006* OSL^2 + .004 CDA − .005 USA
           (.047)   (.002)   (.012)   (.012)
           + Industry Dummies $\bar{R}^2 = .030$; $F(16,733) = 1.59$

(11) AGS   1.088 − .177** OSL + .008** OSL^2 − .041 CDA − .025 USA
           (.109)   (.005)   (.027)   (.026)
           + Industry Dummies $\bar{R}^2 = .033$; $F(16, 733) = 1.57$

(12) AGFA 1.008 − .182** OSL + .009** OSL^2 − .038 CDA − .014 USA
           (.109)   (.005)   (.031)   (.030)
           + Industry Dummies $\bar{R}^2 = .018$; $F(16,733) = .84$

Notes: Industry dummies were not reported in equations (10)-(12) because none were significant, except for petroleum in the case of AGS.

Figures in parentheses are standard errors.
* = significant at 5%.
** = significant at 10%.

size-growth relationship is parabolic, with growth decreasing with size up to a point, and then increasing. Most firms, however, are found in the declining range.[7] The degree of explanatory power of these equations is very weak, indicating that size is not a very powerful determinant of growth. This is particularly so in the cases of AGS and AGFA, where the $\bar{R}^2$'s are so low as to cast doubt on the whole relationship. The F-statistics in these cases suggest that these coefficients are not significant, when considered as a whole.

The heteroscedasticity check revealed that the variance of the growth terms did indeed fluctuate with firm size. This was corrected for in the following manner. It was assumed that the absolute value of the residual of the equation in question was related to the size term in the following way:

$$|residual| = a \cdot S^c,$$

where S = firm size and a is a constant.
Taking logs,

$$\log |residual| = c \cdot \log S + \log a$$

This equation was estimated for each of the three growth equations, (4) to (6), with the resulting c's being: $-.222$ (AGA), $-.149$ (AGS), and $-.166$ (AGFA).

Equations (4) to (6) were then reestimated by weighting each term by $S^c = W$. These equations are numbered (7) to (9) in Table VI-6. These equations confirm that the parabolic relationship is correct.[8] Thus, size negatively affects growth only up to a point. However, the very largest firms grow faster than the next largest firms, although they usually do not grow faster than the mean.

Equations of the type found in Table VI-6 were also estimated by control and industry groups. In the case of the industry groupings, which are not reported, it was found that the size-growth relationship was significant in only two industries, food and beverages, and petroleum. In both cases, the parabolic relationship is reversed: growth increases with size up to a point, and then declines. These equations, however, could not be considered significant when considered as a whole (as indicated by the regression F-statistic). Furthermore, homogeneity tests indicated that pooling by industry was warranted.

Equations (10) to (12) of Table VI-6 estimate the growth equations with the control and industry dummies.[9] It was not deemed necessary to report the industry dummies, since only one was significant, and only in the AGS equation: that being petroleum with a positive

TABLE VI-7

Regression: Growth = a + b_1 Log Opening Size (Assets) + b_2 Log Opening Size (Assets)^2

	Total			U.S.		
	(1) Growth (Assets)	(2) Growth (Sales)	(3) Growth (Fixed) (Assets)	(4)	(5)	(6)
	AGA	AGS	AGFA	AGA	AGS	AGFA
a	.829	1.136	1.042	.841	1.249	.794
b_1	-.140*	-.203*	-.195**	-.143*	-.222*	-.143
	(.045)	(.100)	(.114)	(.056)	(.094)	(.104)
b_2	.006*	.009**	.009**	.006*	.010*	.007
	(.002)	(.005)	(.005)	(.003)	(.004)	(.005)
$\bar{R}^2$	.024	.006	.004	.031	.018	.006
F( )	9.33(2,747)	2.23(2,747)	1.48(2,747)	5.75(2,359)	3.25(2,359)	16.01(2,359)

TABLE VI-7 (cont'd.)

	Other Foreign			Canada		
	(7)	(8)	(9)	(10)	(11)	(12)
	AGA	AGS	AGFA	AGA	AGS	AGFA
a	.007	-2.082	.883	1.034	2.161	1.716
b_1	-.014	.412	-.132	-.179*	-.403*	-.330
	(.152)	(.513)	(.378)	(.083)	(.177)	(.247)
b_2	.001	-.019	.007	.008*	.019*	.016
	(.007)	(.590)	(.018)	(.004)	(.007)	(.012)
$\bar{R}^2$	.001	.009	.003	.029	.020	.006
F( )	.09(2,95)	.43(2,95)	.13(2,95)	4.33(2,287)	2.93(2,287)	.91(2,287)

Notes: * = significant at 5%.

sign. In other words, industry plays no role in determining the level of growth rates. The same is true when country of control is considered, as the control dummies are not significant either. Furthermore, the explanatory power of these equations is very weak, and the F-statistics for the equations indicate that none of these equations' coefficients can be considered significant, taken as a whole. This contrasts sharply with the profitability equations which were highly significant, when industry and control dummies were included.

Even though control exerts no significant impact on the *level* of the growth rate, the pattern of growth differs by control category. Table VI-7 presents the basic growth equation by control group.[10] A casual perusal of these equations seems to suggest that the control groups are not homogeneous, i.e., that the growth equations differ by country of control. This impression is only partially confirmed by the Chow-tests.[11] It has already been noted that the intercepts of the equations cannot be said to differ. The Chow-tests reveal that the slopes do *not* differ in the cases of AGA and AGFA, but do differ in the case of AGS. The source of the difference is the Other Foreign firms in the sample. Nevertheless, in all equations the degree of explanatory power is so weak that the results must be approached with caution.

As a general conclusion, it seems that over-all, larger firms do not grow as rapidly as smaller firms, whatever the definition of growth. The size-growth relationship is best explained by a parabolic function which suggests that growth declines with size only up to a point. Growth rates generally turn up only for the very largest firms. There is a tendency towards regression in firm size. This cannot be interpreted as a movement towards deconcentration in the manufacturing sector since not all firms are included in the sample, and large mergers have not been accounted for. The results remain highly suggestive, nonetheless. When firms are restricted to internal growth, there is no tendency for concentration to increase. This points to the critical role of mergers in increasing aggregate concentration.

Foreign control does not affect either the level or the pattern of growth in most cases. There is a broad tendency for all firms to regress towards the same mean asset size, thus suggesting a tendency for foreign control to decline in this sample, where the largest firms are foreign-controlled. This tendency is mitigated by the lower standard deviation of growth rates of U.S. firms. Again, it must be emphasized that this conclusion holds only for this sample, and for internal growth processes. Mergers, births, and capital inflows are not considered. Furthermore, Other Foreign firms at times display growth characteristics which differ from those of other firms.

Although foreign control cannot be said to have a significant impact on the level of growth rates, it remains true that average Canadian-controlled firms grew faster when assets measure growth, but foreign-controlled firms grew faster according to other measures. This is partially explained by the tendency of Canadian-controlled firms to invest in affiliated firms at a relatively higher rate.

The equations designed to explain inter-firm differences in growth are very weak. It cannot be said that we have succeeded in identifying the determinants of firm growth. Indeed, it appears at this stage as if growth remains, if not a purely random process, then at least one which is largely unexplained, depending somewhat on firm size, and not at all on the country of control or the industry of the firm. This statement is less true for the growth of assets than it is for the growth of sales, which is not surprising given the dependence of the latter on market conditions.

The subsequent sections attempt to further define the growth process by examining other variables which may explain inter-firm differences in growth. The most important of these is profitability.

VI-5 Profitability and Growth: A Note

We have thus far ignored the role of profitability in explaining inter-firm differences in growth rates, and with good reason. For one thing, the relationship between size and profitability suggests that it would be inappropriate to include both variables in the same estimated equation. It is therefore likely that size is acting for profitability in these equations.

Another factor to be considered is the possible identification problem which arises when profitability is used as an independent variable in growth equations. The problem arises because it is not certain whether profitability causes growth or vice-versa. The growth of sales has already been found to be positively related to profitability; firms which are fast-growing in sales will be operating near full-capacity, with the result that profitability is enhanced. The literature on the growth-profitability relationship has concerned itself with equations suggesting that profitability causes growth. A survey of such studies and their rationale may be found in Eatwell (1971).[12] Eatwell's survey is based on the results obtained from regressing a profitability measure on a growth measure, i.e., equations of the basic form,

$$g = a + b\pi + e$$

where g is a growth term, π is a profitability measure and e is an error term. The relationship is usually found to be positive.

Jacquemin and Cardon (1973), in a study of European firms, estimated an equation of the form,

$$g = a + b_1\pi + b_2S + \Sigma c_iI + \Sigma d_iC + u$$

where g and π are as above, S is a size term, and I and C are industry and country dummies. Again, growth and profitability were found to be positively related.

Despite our serious reservations regarding the validity of such equations, they were nonetheless estimated if only to ensure that the relationship also holds for Canada. The estimation procedure involved some problems regarding the choice of variables.

The growth of assets, or perhaps fixed assets, are likely to be more appropriate growth measures, since these are more indicative of the firm's planned expansion. For completeness, the growth of sales terms has been included in the results, but if the above explanation is correct, one would expect the profitability-growth of the sales relationship to be weaker than the relationship between profitability and the growth of assets.

Another problem relates to the choice of the profitability measure. Logically, the appropriate measure should be net of interest and taxes. Both EBIT and GPS are gross of these items. However, EBIT is nearly perfectly collinear with its net variant, and the results therefore do not change. NPK is net of interest and taxes and is included as a profitability measure. GPS is included in recognition of those theories which suggest that firms' mark-ups are determined by the planned expansion of capacity and other assets.

A final consideration must involve the time period. We are measuring growth over an entire period, and it seems unlikely that the closing year's profits will influence the growth rate. Indeed, it may well be that current period growth is determined by profitability in a previous period. We can do no more than mention these problems. Data are not available for a previous period; and there is no a priori method of determining which year's or combination of years' profit rates do affect growth. The latter will doubtless differ from firm to firm according to each one's planning procedures, time horizons, and accounting practices. The average profitability over the period seems to be an adequate index of the firm's long-run relative profitability, and was therefore utilized.[13]

The results of estimating equations of the type mentioned above are presented in Tables VI-8 and VI-9, for all firms. Table VI-8 presents the results obtained from a simple regression of various profitability measures on various growth measures. It can be seen that a positive growth-profitability relationship is confirmed, but the re-

TABLE VI-8

Growth and Profitability: Regression Results, All Firms

$$g = a + b\pi$$

π / g	EBIT			NPK			GPS		
	a	b	$\bar{R}^2$	a	b	$\bar{R}^2$	a	b	$\bar{R}^2$
AGA	.040	.243*	.056	.050	.176*	.049	.051	.062*	.008
		(.036)			(.028)			(.025)	
AGFA	.014	.236*	.009	.030	.097	.006	.015	.101**	.003
		(.093)			(.072)			(.062)	
AGS	.062	.139**	.004	.088	.125*	.005	.043	.149*	.009
		(.082)			(.063)			(.055)	

Notes: * = significant at 5%.
** = significant at 10%.

sults are extremely weak. The strongest relationships, and the only ones which at all provide minimally acceptable degrees of explanation, are those between NPK and AGA, and EBIT and AGA. It was expected that profitability and asset growth would be more closely related than profitability and sales growth. However, the weak explanatory power of the AGFA equations was unexpected.

Table VI-9 presents a selected sample of results obtained by regressing profitability and size on growth. The industry and country of control dummies proved to be insignificant and were therefore excluded from the equations. The equations presented are the best fitting equations.

Profitability retains its positive impact on growth, but the significance of the coefficients considered as a whole cannot be accepted at even 10% confidence limits. This indicates that profitability and size are highly collinear.

In general, profitability and growth have been found to be positively related. However, the explanatory power of profitability as a determinant of growth is weak, and in many cases, very weak. Industry and country of control do not affect the level of growth. It remains true that the determinants of growth are largely unexplained and the growth process may be considered as being essentially random. It is also true that a reduction in *average* profitability would tend to reduce the growth rates of some firms, but only if the reduction is sustained.

VI-6 Other Factors Influencing Firm Growth

The relative inability of the variables thus far considered to explain the growth of firms has led to the tentative conclusion that

TABLE VI-9

GROWTH, PROFITABILITY, AND SIZE: TOTAL SAMPLE, SELECTED EQUATIONS

$$g = a + b_1\pi + b_2S + b_3S^2$$

	a	b_1	b_2	b_3	$\bar{R}^2$	F(3,746)
1. g = growth of assets	.681	.224*	−.119*	.005*	.071	2.19
π = EBIT		(.037)	(.044)	(.002)		
S = log of opening size						
2. g = growth of assets	.738	.168*	−.126*	.006*	.069	1.73
π = NPK		(.028)	(.044)	(.002)		
S = log of opening size						
3. g = growth of fixed assets	.850	.251*	−.158	.007	.025	.64
π = GPS		(.062)	(.113)	(.005)		
S = log of opening size						

Notes: * = significant at 5%.

growth is largely random. There may be other factors, not withstand-
ing, which exert a systematic influence on firm growth which have
not been considered. As a consequence, other variables were examined in relation to the growth of the firm. As it turns out, none were
successful in further explaining inter-firm differences in growth.
Some of the tests undertaken are summarized in this section.

Amongst the variables considered were the assets/sales ratio, the
fixed assets/sales ratio, the ratio of labour costs to total costs, and the
leverage ratio. The first three were employed as possible proxies for
capital intensity, because it could be argued that high capital intensity impedes growth owing to the large investments required. No evidence could be found to support this idea, as none of the capital intensity variables were able to add to the explanatory power of the
growth equations.

It might be argued that it is not absolute capital intensity which
serves as a barrier to growth, but rather marginal capital intensity,
i.e., the additional capital required to finance an additional unit of
sales. Thus the variable of interest would be the incremental capital-
output ratio. Firms with higher incremental capital-output ratios
would require larger investments in order to grow. This measure
could not be calculated in a precise way since it would require time-
series data for each firm. However, following Filippi and Zanetti
(1971), the following equations were estimated by size and control
group:

$$\text{Average Assets} = a + b_1 \text{ Average Sales}$$
$$\text{Average Fixed Assets} = a + b_1 \text{ Average Sales}$$

The estimated coefficients b_1 represent the cross-section incremental capital-output ratios, while the constant a may be thought of
as the minimal asset requirement for the category. One would expect
the b's to increase with increasing firm size if the above argument is
correct. No such tendency was found. Only for the very largest firms
(with assets exceeding $160 million) was the estimated b found to be
significantly greater than that estimated for other size groups. No
difference was found between foreign- and Canadian-controlled
firms. Thus, over-all, the growth performance of firms seems to be
unrelated to marginal capital intensity, except perhaps in the case of
the very largest firms.

Leverage was considered as a determinant of firm growth on the
grounds that highly levered firms might find it difficult to raise
funds for further expansion. Alternatively it could be argued that
highly levered firms are more concerned with growth, and attempt
to achieve high rates of growth through borrowing. No significant

growth-leverage relationship was found, for any definition of leverage or growth.

Finally, the relationship between profits and investment in plant and equipment was considered. The growth process is clearly related to the investment process, and while a detailed investigation of the latter is beyond the scope of this study, a few observations are possible. Table VI-10 presents the five-year average of plant and equipment expenditures as a proportion of the five-year average net profits, by size and control groups. This ratio reflects, albeit imperfectly, the degree to which firms re-invest their net profits. The measure is imperfect since plant and investment expenditures tend to be non-continuous and there is no guarantee that the five-year period considered here is representative of a firm's investment behaviour. In addition, there is no necessary one-to-one correspondence between profits and investment over the same time period. Nevertheless, assuming that such biases affect all groups in the same way, some comparisons are possible. It can be seen that there is no particular relationship between the investment ratio and firm size, a conclusion which was confirmed by regression analysis.[14] The ratio is certainly smallest for the very largest firms, particularly when they are foreign-controlled. Indeed, the most interesting aspect of Table VI-10 is that foreign-controlled firms in general, but particularly U.S.-controlled firms, re-invested a lower percentage of their profits over the period. Regression analysis confirmed that the level of the

TABLE VI-10

Average Expenditures on Plant and Equipment as a Proportion of Average Net Profits, by Size and Control Groups

Size Category (000,000)	U.S.		OF		CAN	
	(a)	(b)	(a)	(b)	(a)	(b)
<5	.66	.66	X	X	1.59	1.59
5-10	1.00	1.81	−5.84	7.33	1.88	3.03
10-20	2.04	3.49	1.75	2.13	3.52	6.75
20-40	1.60	2.20	−.62	2.40	1.66	3.45
40-80	1.64	1.76	.59	2.50	2.26	6.06
80-160	1.69	1.89	−.61	2.57	1.00	1.25
>160	1.05	1.17	.66	.66	.54	1.88
TOTAL	1.41	2.15	−1.13	3.54	1.96	3.87

Notes: (a) includes loss corporations
       (b) excludes loss corporations
       X: omitted to preserve confidentiality

U.S. firms' ratio was significantly lower than that of either Canadian or Other Foreign firms.[15] It will be recalled that U.S.-controlled firms also tend to borrow less money, thus implying that they mobilized fewer funds for investment in plant and equipment over the period.

The attempt to isolate other firm-specific factors which influence firm growth must be judged a failure. The significant conclusion to emerge from this section is that U.S.-controlled firms did not re-invest as high as proportion of their profits as did other firms. Combined, our results suggest that while there is a random component to growth processes, the specific behaviour of U.S.-controlled firms may influence their growth. In general, however, it would seem that the determinants of growth are not micro-economic.

VI-7 Summary and Conclusions

This chapter has concerned itself with a comparison of the level and pattern of growth of foreign- and Canadian-controlled firms. The results are somewhat surprising. In spite of the fact that U-S.-controlled firms are more profitable, and in spite of the positive relationship between growth and profitability, it cannot be said that U.S.-controlled grew significantly faster than other firms, for any measure of growth. Indeed, the growth rates of all control groups cannot be said to differ statistically from each other, although they do differ. In addition, there is a tendency for all firms to regress towards the same mean growth rate. This implies that the growth process is the same for all control groups. In general, the growth process is not well explained by micro-economic factors such as firm size, profitability, industry or country of control. Although smaller firms do tend to grow faster than larger firms, the explanatory power of this relationship is weak. The growth process cannot be described as being completely random, but it is certainly largely unexplained.

The interpretation of these results, both with respect to foreign ownership and control, and with respect to more general consider-ations, is not easy. It would appear that all firms, with the possible exception of Other Foreign firms, conform to the same growth process which may be broadly characterized as being independent of firm-specific factors. The exact factors which do determine growth remain unexplained, and may be broadly characterized as being random, in the sense that many factors in the firm's economic environment are responsible for its growth performance. Our a priori expectation was that the subsidiaries of foreign firms would respond to a broader economic environment defined by the international net-work of their multinational parents, whereas domestic firms would respond only to their immediate economic environment, the national economy of Canada. In this scenario, the effects of firm-specific variables on the growth of foreign-controlled firms might be expected to be weaker, since the growth decision is based on the international position of the firm. This has not proved to be the case.

Nevertheless, one cannot comfortably assert that the determinants of growth are the same for all firms. For one thing, firms may indeed be responding to economic environments, the sum of whose effects produces a large random component in the growth process, but which are nevertheless qualitatively different. The fact that U.S.-controlled firms were found to be more profitable, and that they tended to re-invest a lower percentage of their profits in plant and equipment leaves one suspicious of any strong conclusion regarding the similarity of the growth processes of Canadian- and U.S.-controlled firms. In the case of Other Foreign-controlled firms, it has been found that on average they exhibit high growth rates of sales and fixed assets, although these were not found to be statistically higher than those of other firms. In several cases, however, the slopes of OF equations were found to differ from the other groups. It would appear that Other Foreign firms were engaged in many new investment projects and were at an early stage of the product cycle. Because these are characteristics common to younger firms, it could therefore be suggested that Other Foreign firms differ from other firms on this basis and not on the basis of multinationality. Again, we conclude that foreign-controlled firms differ from each other, although the difference is not as pronounced as that for profitability and financial structure.

On a more general level, our results point to the crucial role of competition policy, particularly with respect to mergers, in reducing aggregate concentration. In the absence of mergers and new entrants, it is clear that a process of deconcentration would occur. The recent Royal Commission on Corporate Concentration found that there has been no such trend since 1966, thus suggesting that mergers have retarded the process. Any attempt to reduce aggregate concentration must begin with a policy towards mergers.

Notes

1. The growth rate of net fixed assets was also calculated, but no difference in the reported results occurs, partly because no difference in reported depreciation rates could be found among firms of different size or control groups.

2. Variants, such as the Yule or Pareto distributions, are often used in this context.

3. For a thorough, non-technical introduction to *Gibrat's Law*, see Prais (1976). He uses the term "spontaneous drift" to describe the phenomenon.

4. See Prais (1976, Chapter 2) for an excellent discussion of these conditions.

5. Since the Spearman coefficients are calculated by ranking the two sets of variables, the degree of association between a growth rate and size, whether calculated in absolute or logarithmic terms, will be the same. This is so because the logarithmic transformation changes the magnitude but not the ordering of the size variable.

6. Other things are not quite equal, however. The standard deviation of growth rates for U.S.-controlled is lower than that for Canadian-controlled firms. This would tend to limit the tendency for the U.S. share to decline.

7. The turning points implied by these equations are (approximately).
    AGA: 120 million dollars (assets)
    AGS: 80 million dollars (assets)
    AGFA: 50 million dollars (assets)

8. Equations (7) to (9), while providing different coefficients, yield the same information as equations (4) to (6). The turning point is precisely the same in each comparable case.

9. These equations are not weighted since the weighting procedure is not appropriate in a regression with both continuous and dummy variables. There seems no reason to believe that weighting would change the results, given that the number of observations is reasonably large. See Theil (1971, pp. 243 ff.)

10. The estimated equations for the total sample are repeated in Table VI-7 in order to facilitate comparisons. The unweighted versions are presented for simplicity. The results are not changed when the equations are weighted.

11. The Chow tests were based on unweighted equations. See footnote 9.

12. Profitability is assumed to cause growth because profitability is seen as a source of investment funds, i.e., the relationship is viewed from the supply of funds side. While this view appears to be reasonable, it does assume, taken alone, that the only constraint to the growth of the firm is the ability to finance it, which in turn suggests that cost curves never turn up. However, even if one finds that profitability is positively related to growth, one cannot conclude that the causality runs from profitability to growth because of the identification problem. See Radice (1971).

13. Experiments with other frameworks (the average profitability over the first three years of the period, or the opening profitability) revealed no important differences from the reported results.

14. Negative numbers in Table VI-10 result from firms which, on average, incurred losses over the period. This problem distorts the meaning of

the figures, particularly for Other Foreign firms. As a consequence, the investment ratio was calculated using only firms which made positive five-year profits. The conclusions are not dependent on the measure employed.

15. The regression equation included the industry dummy variables, none of which were significant.

VII

CONCLUSION

This study has concerned itself with a comparison of the financial structure and performance of foreign- and Canadian-controlled manufacturing firms in Canada. Recent literature on the multinational corporation has suggested that the nature of the MNC is such that its subsidiaries operating abroad will exhibit characteristics which differ systematically from those of primarily domestic firms. It is within the framework of this literature that the comparative analysis has been undertaken.

The purpose of this chapter is to bring together the empirical findings and conclusions presented in the preceding chapters and to interpret their relevance, both to the theory of the multinational firm and to the ongoing debate over foreign ownership of the Canadian economy. It should be noted at the outset, however, that the limited objectives of this study necessarily preclude an over-all assessment of the costs and benefits of foreign ownership in Canada. Nor will all the results and conclusions which have been previously summarized be repeated here.

The results clearly indicated that when firms were grouped by country of control, and when other factors were held constant, important differences in financial structure and profitability emerged between and among the control groups. All firms operating in Canada cannot be said to have represented a homogeneous group; foreign control does make a difference. Nevertheless, it is equally inappropriate to view all foreign-controlled firms as being similar. Firms controlled in countries other than the U.S. or Canada exhibited characteristics which sometimes differed from those of other firms, be they U.S.- or Canadian-controlled, but which often were closer to those exhibited by Canadian-controlled firms.

While many, but not all, of the differences between U.S.- and Canadian-controlled firms are consistent with hypotheses drawn from theories regarding the nature of MNCs, it is difficult to reconcile the observed differences between U.S.- and Other Foreign-controlled firms on these grounds. For example, U.S.-controlled firms have been found to be the least highly levered group in Canada, while Other Foreign firms have been found to be the most highly levered. This result is consistent with national borrowing practices in Europe and the U.S., and it might therefore be suggested that national, as opposed to multinational, financial practices were the cause of the difference. On the other hand, the tendency of U.S.-controlled firms to borrow more heavily from affiliated firms implies that they had greater access to an internal network of financial resources; this is certainly consistent with the notion that MNCs rely on an integrated system of financing. Similarly, the higher liquidity of U.S.-controlled firms, which was caused by higher inventories, is consistent with the idea that the integration of firms' transactions across national borders requires the security of extra stocks. On balance, it would seem that subsidiaries of U.S.-based parents were the only foreign-controlled firms in Canada which can be said to have exhibited characteristics associated with integrated, multinational financial operations.

The same is true of profitability. Only U.S.-controlled firms claimed a profitability premium above and beyond that associated with other firms in the same broad industry, of the same size, and with the same degree of market power. Indeed, there was no evidence that U.S.-controlled firms in this sample were either larger, or over-represented in highly concentrated industries, according to the measures employed. The profitability advantage of U.S.-controlled firms could be explained by their access to assets monopolized internally by their parents, and which were not available to other firms. These assets may include such things as products, processes, goodwill, or management techniques. Other Foreign-controlled firms cannot be said to have enjoyed such advantages. Furthermore, the more highly foreign-owned was the U.S.-controlled firm, the more profitable was it likely to be. The reverse was true of Other Foreign-controlled firms, thus suggesting that the advantage of U.S.-controlled firms was indeed internal to the firm, and is best exploited by tight control. Again, characteristics associated with "multinationality" were exhibited only by firms controlled by U.S. parents. It might be argued that Other Foreign-controlled firms moved abroad in response to the "American Challenge" without possessing those features which made U.S. firms multinational in the first place. The possession of a unique asset may thus be viewed as a sufficient, but not a necessary condition for the movement abroad. Conditions of oligopolistic competition must also be considered. But it could also be argued that Other Foreign firms possessed, but did not manifest, characteristics of multinationality, and that they will do so in time. Over the relatively short period considered here, this did not happen. Profitability, and profitability differentials by control group, tended to persist over the period.

Although no a priori theory was advanced regarding the stability of profitability of foreign-controlled firms, the results have indicated that U.S.-controlled firms exhibited greater stability. While many explanations for this finding could no doubt be offered, it is not inconsistent with other results. If anything, it strengthens the view that subsidiaries of U.S.-based parents possess unique advantages in product development, marketing, financial planning and perhaps pricing. All of these advantages may be linked to the ability of such firms to integrate operations across borders.

Firm growth has been characterized as being a largely random process for all firms, regardless of country of control. Country of control has not been found to affect the rate at which firms grew. Yet it cannot be categorically stated that the underlying growth process was the same for all firms, i.e., that the ability of multinational firms, particularly if U.S.-based, to centralize funds and activities does not affect the growth of its subsidiaries. There is some evidence to support the view that the growth of U.S.-controlled firms was in fact truncated. U.S.-controlled firms invested less in affiliated companies, spent less on non-production labour, invested less of their profits in plant and equipment, and despite their higher profitability, did not grow significantly faster than other firms. Again, Other Foreign-controlled firms were not found to share these characteristics.

It may be concluded, therefore, that there is considerable evidence which suggests that the subsidiaries of foreign-based, and presumably multinational, parents operating in Canada are different from domestic firms, but only if the former are subsidiaries of U.S.-based parents. Those features hypothesized to be characteristic of subsidiaries of MNCs were generally found to have applied only to U.S.-controlled firms in Canada. The implications of this result, while suggestive, cannot be fully explored until further evidence is accumulated in other countries and for other time periods.

The results obtained here possess more than theoretical implications. They suggest that various economic policies may have a differential impact on Canadian- and foreign-controlled firms, particularly if the latter are U.S.-controlled. Uniformly applied economic policies may provoke different reactions, or produce different results, depending on which control group is being considered. Furthermore, some policies which might be thought to be neutral in terms of foreign ownership may, on the contrary, have implications for future trends in foreign ownership.

Deflationary fiscal and monetary policies are likely to affect Canadian-controlled firms, and possibly Other Foreign-controlled firms, more than they affect U.S.-controlled firms. The latter have been found to be more liquid and to rely less on borrowed funds, indicating that such firms are less dependent on creditors and are less susceptible to credit squeezes brought on by high interest rates and/or deteriorating market conditions. These factors, in combination with the internal sources of credit to which U.S.-controlled firms apparently have access, clearly puts them in an advantageous position in periods of recession. The evidence has shown that U.S.-controlled firms were more successful in maintaining profit rates and margins during periods of economic contraction, and were less likely to incur losses. These factors contributed to the greater stability of profitability which was observed for U.S.-controlled firms.

In general, Canadian-controlled firms were found to have been less profitable, less financially sound, and less stable than similarly placed U.S.-controlled firms. These characteristics, should they persist, make Canadian-controlled firms more susceptible to bankruptcy, or take-over, perhaps by financially stronger U.S.-controlled firms. Such events would appear to be more likely when deflationary policies are in place.

The behaviour of profit rates and margins over the business cycle raises another issue. The fact that U.S.-controlled firms were more successful in protecting their profits during economic contractions has obvious implications for any programme of profit controls. If, for example, profits are frozen at trough-year levels, then Canadian-controlled firms are likely to be relatively disadvantaged. Even if an extended base period is employed, the choice of its length will be important, as will be the phases of the business cycle which it encompasses. The higher temporal variability of profitability of Canadian-controlled firms does suggest that more of them would be "caught" by profit controls.

The results are troublesome with respect to current thinking on industrial structure and the rationalization of Canadian industry. There is certainly independent evidence to support the view that the small size of the Canadian market, perhaps in combination with the miniature replica effect produced by foreign ownership, results in plants which are, if not too small, then at least insufficiently specialized to be efficient. One solution to this problem would allow firms producing similar products to merge, even if industrial concentration is increased, in order to realize economies of scale and specialization at the plant level. The results of this study suggest that a relaxed policy towards mergers, even when increased specialization results, should be approached with caution. Although the full range of potential advantages to large firm size has not been analysed, the evidence suggests that at the firm level, advantages to size exist only for the very largest firms, particularly when foreign-controlled. For Canadian-controlled firms, profit rates declined continuously with size, indicating that the creation of larger Canadian-controlled firms is not necessarily advantageous. Foreign-controlled firms would seem to be better placed to take advantage of an environment which does not restrain merger activity. The creation of larger foreign-controlled firms will result in a redistribution of income and resources to the foreign-owned sector.

While profitability and growth were found to have been positively related, the explanatory power of the relationship was weak. Firm growth was not well explained by the micro-economic variables considered, and it may be suggested that firm growth is explained by a broad range of factors best described as macro-economic. If this is in fact the case, it follows that policy measures designed to foster growth are most efficaciously undertaken at the macro-level. Specifically, policies directed at enhancing firm profitability as a means of encouraging more rapid growth may not be uniformly successful, at least in the absence of the correct macro-environment.

Another problem which arises in this context relates to the growth performance of U.S.-controlled firms. These firms, which experienced above average profitability, did not translate this into above average expansion of assets. Any policy designed to enhance the profitability of such firms runs the risk of seeing these funds used for purposes other than expansion. In addition, there is no guarantee that foreign-controlled firms will respond to favourable aggregate economic conditions in Canada since their reference point may be international, and only the relative behaviour of the Canadian economy would be relevant.

Policies designed to increase Canadian ownership in U.S.-controlled firms are likely to be resisted, since the profit rates of such firms were higher, the lower was the degree of Canadian ownership. However, Other Foreign-controlled firms are likely to encourage Canadian ownership, since Canadian participation enhanced their profitability. Attempts to channel foreign capital into minority ownership of Canadian-controlled firms, while perhaps desirable for some reasons, cannot be justified on the grounds that it will enhance the profitability performance of the firm, unless accompanied by a transfer of resources, such as technology. Thus, it is doubtful whether attempts to change the degree of foreign ownership in Canada via policies involving minority equity participation by either Canadian or foreign investors would meet with much success.

All things taken together, it is evident that no analysis of the Canadian economy can be undertaken which ignores the presence of foreign-controlled firms. The behaviour and performance of foreign-controlled firms in Canada, particularly those controlled from the U.S., is sufficiently different as to warrant continued research into their role in Canadian economic life.

Bibliography

Baldwin, W. L., "Industrial Structure, Size and Rates of Return Among Fortune's 500," *Industrial Organization Review* 2, 1974, pp. 169-185.

Berle, A., and Means, G. C., *The Modern Corporation and Private Property*, New York, 1932.

Berlin, P. D., *Foreign Affiliate Financial Survey*, 1966-69, U.S. Department of Commerce, Office of Foreign Direct Investments, Washington, 1971.

Bertin, G. Y., "Foreign Expansion and Diversification of Multinational Firms," in G. Paquet (editor), *The Multinational Firm and the Nation State*, Collier-Macmillan, Toronto, 1972.

Bloch, H., "Prices, Costs and Profits in Canadian Manufacturing: The Influence of Tariffs and Concentration," *Canadian Journal of Economics* 7, Nov. 1974, pp. 594-610.

Brash, D., *American Investment in Australian Industry*, Harvard University Press, 1966.

Canada, *Foreign Ownership and the Structure of Canadian Industry* (The Watkins Report), Ottawa, 1968.

Canada, *Foreign Direct Investment in Canada* (The Gray Report), Ottawa, 1972.

Carter, J. R., "In Search of Synergy: A Structure-Performance Test," *Review of Economics and Statistics*, 59, August 1977, pp. 279-289.

Caves, R. E., "International Corporations: The Industrial Economics of Foreign Investment," *Economica* 38, February 1971, pp. 1-27.

———, "Causes of Direct Investment: Foreign Firms' Share of Canadian and United Kingdom Manufacturing Industries," *Review of Economics and Statistics*, 56, August 1974, pp. 279-293.

———, *Diversification, Foreign Investment and Scale in North American Manufacturing Industries*, Economic Council of Canada, Ottawa, 1975.

Clark, J. J., Clark, M. T., and Elgers, P. T., *Financial Management: A Capital Market Approach*, Holbrook Press, Boston, 1976.

Coutinho, L., "The Internationalization of Oligopoly Capital," unpublished doctoral dissertation, Cornell University, 1975.

Demsetz, H., "Two Systems of Belief About Monopoly," in H. Goldschmid et al. (editors), *Industrial Concentration: The New Learning*, Little, Brown, Boston, 1974, pp. 164-183.

Dennis, K., "Market Power and the Behaviour of Industrial Prices," in Prices and Incomes Commission, *Essays on Price Changes*, Ottawa, 1973.

Draper, N. R., and Smith, H., *Applied Regression Analysis*, John Wiley, New York, 1966.

Dunning, J., "U.S. Subsidiaries in Britain and Their U.K. Competitors," *Business Ratios*, Autumn 1966.

————, "The Determinants of International Production," *Oxford Economic Papers* 25, November 1973, pp. 289-336.

Eastman, H. and Stykolt, S., *The Tariff and Competition in Canada*, Macmillan, Toronto, 1967.

Eatwell, J., "Growth, Profitability and Size: The Empirical Evidence," in R. Marris and A. Wood (editors), *The Corporate Economy*, Macmillan, New York, 1971.

Economic Council of Canada, *Looking Outward*, Ottawa, 1975.

Eichner, A., "A Theory of the Determination of the Mark-up Under Oligopoly," *Economic Journal* 83, December 1973, pp. 1184-2000.

Gale, B. T., "Market Share and Rate of Return," *Review of Economics and Statistics* 54, November 1972, pp. 412-423.

Globerman, S., "Foreign Direct Investment and 'Spillover' Efficiency Benefits in Canadian Manufacturing Industries," *Canadian Journal of Economics* 12, February 1979, pp. 42-56.

Gupta, M. C., "The Effect of Size, Growth and Industry on the Financial Structure of Manufacturing Companies," *Journal of Finance* 24, June 1969, pp. 517-529.

Hall, M., and Weiss, L., "Firm Size and Profitability," *Review of Economics and Statistics*, 49, August, 1967, pp. 319-331.

Hinchcliff, R., and Shapiro, D., "Corporate Take-Overs in Canada, 1968-1973," mimeo, Statistics Canada, 1975.

Howe, J. D., and McFetridge, D., "The Determinants of R & D Expenditures," *Canadian Journal of Economics* 9, February 1976, pp. 57-71.

Hurdle, G., "Leverage, Market Structure, and Profitability," *Review of Economics and Statistics,* 56, February 1974, pp. 478-485.

Hymer, S., "The International Operations of National Firms: A Study of Direct Investment," doctoral dissertation, MIT, 1960.

Jacquemin, A., and Cardon de Lichtbuer, M., "Size Structure, Stability, and Performance of the Largest British and EEC Firms," *European Economic Review* 4, December 1973, pp. 393-408.

Jacquemin, A. and deJong, H. W., *European Industrial Organization,* John Wiley and Sons, New York, 1977.

Jenny, F., and Weber, A. P., "Taux de Profit et Variables Structurelles," *Revue Économique* 6, Novembre 1974, pp. 924-958.

Johnson, W. B., "The Cross-Sectional Stability of Financial Patterns," *Journal of Business Finance and Accounting* 5, 2, 1978, pp. 207-214.

Johnston, J., *Econometric Methods* (second edition), McGraw-Hill, New York, 1972.

Jones, J. C. H., Laudadio, L., and Percy, M., "Market Structure and Profitability in Canadian Manufacturing Industry," *Canadian Journal of Economics* 6, August 1973, pp. 356-368.

Knickerbocker, F. T., *Oligopolistic Reaction and the Multinational Enterprise,* Harvard University Press, 1973.

Lall, S., "Transnationals, Domestic Enterprises and Industrial Structure in Host LDCs: A Survey," *Oxford Economic Papers* 30, July 1978, pp. 217-248.

Leftwich, R., "U.S. Multinational Companies: Profitability, Financial Leverage, and Effective Tax Rates," *Survey of Current Business,* May 1974.

Marcus, M., "Profitability and Size of Firm: Some Further Evidence," *Review of Economics and Statistics* 51, February 1969, pp. 217-224.

McFetridge, D., "Market Structure and Price-Cost Margins: An Analysis of the Canadian Manufacturing Sector," *Canadian Journal of Economics* 6, August 1973, pp. 344-355.

McFetridge, D., and Weatherley, L. J., *Notes on the Economics of*

Large Firm Size, Royal Commission on Corporate Concentration Study No. 20, Ottawa, 1977.

Modigliani, F., and Miller, M., "The Cost of Capital, Corporation Finance, and the Theory of Investment," *American Economic Review* 48, June 1958, pp. 261-297.

Naumann-Etienne, R., "A Framework for Financial Decisions in Multinational Corporations," *Journal of Financial and Quantitative Analysis,* November 1974, pp. 859-874.

Orr, D., "An Index of Entry Barriers and its Application to the Market Structure-Performance Relationship," *The Journal of Industrial Economics* 22, September 1974, pp. 39-49.

_____, "The Industrial Composition of U.S. Exports and Subsidiary Sales to the Canadian Market: Comment," *American Economic Review* 65, March 1975, pp. 230-234.

Parry, T. G., "Plant Size, Capacity Utilization and Economic Efficiency: Foreign Investment in the Australian Chemical Industry," *Economic Record* 50, June 1974, pp. 218-244.

Pattison, J. C., *Financial Markets and Foreign Ownership,* Ontario Economic Council, Occasional Paper 8, Toronto, 1978.

Porter, M., "Consumer Behaviour, Retailer Power and Market Performance in Consumer Goods Industries," *Review of Economics and Statistics* 56, November 1974, pp. 419-436.

Prachowny, M., and Richardson, J. D., "Testing a Life-Cycle Hypothesis of the Balance of Payments Effects of Multinational Corporations," *Economic Enquiry,* 13, March 1975, pp. 81-98.

Prais, S. J., "The Statistical Conditions for a Change in Business Concentration," *Review of Economics and Statistics* 40, August 1958, pp. 268-273.

_____, *The Evolution of Giant Firms in Britain,* Cambridge University Press, 1976.

Radice, H., "Control Type, Profitability and Growth in Large Firms: An Empirical Study," *Economic Journal* 81, September 1971, pp. 547-549.

Robbins, S., and Stobaugh, R., *Money in the Multinational Enterprise,* Basic Books, New York, 1973.

Rosenbluth, G., "The Relation Between Foreign Control and Concentration in Canadian Industry," *Canadian Journal of Economics* 3, February 1970, pp. 14-38.

Rowthorn, R., and Hymer, S., *International Big Business 1957-1967*, Cambridge University Press, 1971.

Safarian, A. E., *Foreign Ownership of Canadian Industry*, McGraw-Hill, Toronto, 1966.

_____, *The Performance of Foreign-Owned Firms in Canada*, Canadian-American Committee, Montreal, 1969.

Scherer, F., *Industrial Market Structure and Economic Performance*, Rand McNally, Chicago, 1970.

_____, "The Determinants of Industrial Plant Sizes in Six Nations," *Review of Economics and Statistics* 55, May 1973, pp. 135-143.

Shapiro, D., "Multinational Investment and the Canadian Economy," doctoral dissertation, Cornell University, 1974.

Shepherd, W. G., "The Elements of Market Structure," *Review of Economics and Statistics* 54, February 1972, pp. 25-37.

Singh, A. and Whittington, G., *Growth, Profitability, and Valuation* Cambridge University Press, 1968.

Statistics Canada, *Corporations and Labour Unions Returns Act* (CALURA), annual reports, Ottawa.

_____, *Industrial Organization and Concentration in the Manufacturing, Mining and Logging Industries* (31-514), Ottawa, 1972.

Theil, H., *Principles of Econometrics*, Wiley, New York, 1971.

Toy, N.; Stonehill, A.; Remmers, L.; Wright, R. and Beckhuisen, T., "A Comparative International Study of Growth, Profitability and Risk as Determinants of Corporate Debt Ratios in the Manufacturing Sector," *Journal of Financial and Quantitative Analysis*, November 1974, pp. 875-886.

Weiss, L., "The Concentration-Profits Relationship and Anti-Trust," in H. Goldschmid et al. (editors), *Industrial Concentration: The New Learning*, Little, Brown, Boston, 1974, pp. 184-232.

Whittington, G., *The Prediction of Profitability*, Cambridge University Press, 1971.

Wolf, B., "Industrial Diversification and Internationalization: Some Empirical Evidence," *Journal of Industrial Economics* 26, December 1977, pp. 177-191.

Wood, A., *A Theory of Profits*, Cambridge University Press, 1975.

Zietlin, M., "Corporate Ownership and Control," *American Journal of Sociology*, March 1974, pp. 1073-1119.

Index